Richard Chenevix Trench

Sermons New And Old

Archbishop

Richard Chenevix Trench

Sermons New And Old
Archbishop

ISBN/EAN: 9783744743532

Printed in Europe, USA, Canada, Australia, Japan

Cover: Foto ©Lupo / pixelio.de

More available books at **www.hansebooks.com**

SERMONS

NEW AND OLD

BY

RICHARD CHENEVIX TRENCH, D.D.

ARCHBISHOP

LONDON
KEGAN PAUL, TRENCH, & CO., 1 PATERNOSTER SQUARE
1886

CONTENTS.

SERMON		PAGE
I.	Elijah's Translation and Christ's Ascension.	1
II.	Agrippa	11
III.	The Woman that was a Sinner	23
IV.	Joseph and his Brethren	37
V.	Bearing one another's Burdens	50
VI.	The Love of Money.	60
VII.	The Armour of God	71
VIII.	The Thorn in the Flesh	86
IX.	Isaiah's Vision	98
X.	Selfishness	112
XI.	On the Duty of hating vain Thoughts	123
XII.	Pontius Pilate	134
XIII.	The Death and Burial of Moses	152
XIV.	Every Good Gift from above	163
XV.	On the Hearing of Prayer	184
XVI.	The Kingdom which cometh not with Observation	196

SERMON		PAGE
XVII.	PRESSING TOWARD THE MARK	207
XVIII.	THE VALLEY OF DRY BONES	219
XIX.	ALL SAINTS	232
XX.	THE HOLY WOMEN AT THE CROSS	241
XXI.	CHRIST POOR THAT WE MIGHT BE RICH	249
XXII.	LOT'S CHOICE	258
XXIII.	THE STUDY OF SCRIPTURE	267
XXIV.	BAXTER AND 'THE SAINT'S REST'	279

SERMON I.[1]

ELIJAH'S TRANSLATION AND CHRIST'S ASCENSION.

2 KINGS ii. 11.

And it came to pass, as they still went on, and talked, that, behold, there appeared a chariot of fire, and horses of fire, and parted them both asunder; and Elijah went up by a whirlwind into heaven.

THERE is almost nothing in the New Testament, altogether abrupt, altogether unprepared, wholly unlike to all that in the Old went before it. There are few of the leading events of our Lord's life that have not their nearer or remoter analogies, parallels, prefigurations in the lives of some one or more of the Old-Testament saints; God in this fact testifying that He is the author of both Covenants; one purpose, one scheme, one intention running through both, knitting them together, so that it is impossible to detach them from one another, to ascribe divine authority to the one, and at the same time to withhold it from the other. To give an instance of what I mean: there is an anticipation, a feeble one indeed, but still an anticipation, of the Transfiguration

[1] Ascension Day.

of Christ in the skin of Moses' face shining, as he also came down from the mountain where he had been talking with God.¹ The glory, indeed, of Moses' Transfiguration, if we may call it by so august a name, was infinitely less than the glory of Christ's; but this only agreed with the relative position of the two—Moses a servant in the house of another, Christ a Son in his own.

Not otherwise the Ascension of the Lord is prefigured, foreshown, and, we may say, anticipated in part, by the Translation of Elijah; and the Church has marked her sense of the inner connexion in which the two events stand to one another by appointing the chapter from which my text is drawn, the chapter which records the fact and the manner of Elijah's taking up into heaven, as one of the lessons to be read in the services appointed for Ascension Day. We may expect to find, in comparing the two narratives, points of likeness, and points of difference: points of likeness, for the kingdom of God is one, one throughout all ages; its leading events, therefore, will repeat themselves again and again: points of difference, because there is growth in it, advance, development; the bud passes into the flower, the shadow into the substance, the type into the antitype, and God, who spake long and often by his servants, speaks at last by his Son. Nor will such an

¹ Exod. xxxiv. 29.

expectation as this be disappointed. There is already much of Christ's Ascension in Elijah's Translation; but at the same time there are features in the later and more glorious event which exist not at all, or only in their weak outlines, in the earlier: there are points of unlikeness, even of absolute contrast between the one and the other. Let us a little consider that earlier event, Elijah's Translation, to-day, reading it as we go along in the light thrown back upon it by the later, by the Ascension namely of the Lord of glory.

Now at last Elijah's work is done; his long controversy with Israel, with an apostate king and a rebellious people, is drawing to a close; he shall no longer prophesy as in sackcloth, denouncing heavy things to his people,—shutting up heaven with a word, withholding for long years the rain and the dew from the earth,—slaying the wicked prophets of Baal; a man of peace, yet by a stern necessity bringing a sword. All this has ended now. It has been revealed to him that his warfare is accomplished; his rest and reward are near. He shall be withdrawn in a wonderful way from the earth. And his faithful servant Elisha, he too knows what is at hand, cleaves to his lord with a clinging affection: 'As the Lord liveth, and as thy soul liveth, I will not leave thee.' He counts, and rightly, that there will be some boon and blessing for him, some legacy of love, if only he be with his master to the last, and behold him in the very moment of his departure. The pertinacity of his faith at length meets with its reward. Elijah no longer seeks to dismiss him; on the contrary, suggests to him that he should put himself in the way of a blessing, 'Ask what I shall do for thee before I be taken away from thee;' whereupon the longing desire and expectation of Elisha's soul clothe themselves in this petition : ' I pray thee, let a double portion of thy spirit be upon me.'

These words, I would observe by the way, have been often misunderstood, as though Elisha had claimed twice as much of the spirit as that portion which Elijah had for his own. Now none could impart more than he actually possessed—as much perhaps as he possessed, or a part of what he possessed, but certainly not more. Neither does Elisha ask more. All that he asks is, to be recognized as Elijah's eldest-born; that to him, among the spiritual sons of the prophet, the rights of primogeniture might pertain. It was a part of these rights, of the privileges of an eldest son, that the father might bequeath, or indeed was bound to bequeath, to him a double portion of his inheritance, twice as much as he bequeathed to any other;[1] and it is this, not a portion twice as much as Elijah himself actually had, that Elisha sought. The whole course of the after history would, indeed, sufficiently refute

[1] Deut. xxi. 17.

this latter interpretation; for, even granting that the miracles of Elisha are more in number than those of Elijah, and appeal is sometimes made to this fact, yet none who reads this history with any true insight can deny that in Elijah we have the loftier figure, the more heroic nature, the more predominant spirit; that Elisha, the scholar, might indeed carry on the work which Elijah, the master, had auspicated and begun, might complete, but could scarcely have commenced, that great, and in many respects most successful, protest against idolatry which his mightier precursor was first raised up to bear.

But in all this story a higher meaning is ever present with us as we read. We read of Elijah, but we feel that a greater than Elijah is here. Our thoughts carry us on to One who, like the prophet of the elder dispensation, had finished the work upon earth which his Father had given him to do; who had borne the burden and the heat of a yet fiercer day than the prophet had ever borne, endured with a diviner patience, with not even one passing movement of impatience, a worse contradiction of sinners, had drunk the cup of a bitterer agony, had been baptized with the baptism of a more searching pain; and who, now about to leave the earth, announced to his faithful disciples that legacy of love, that promise of the Father, that double portion of the Spirit, which He would bequeath to them, and which should compensate them for his bodily absence in those coming times when they should behold no more Him whom the heavens had received out of their sight.

The actual translation of Elijah follows, being recorded in those words which I have put forward as central to the work of this day: 'And it came to pass, that as they still went on, and talked, that, behold, there appeared a chariot of fire, and horses of fire, and parted them both asunder; and Elijah went up by a whirlwind into heaven.' Compare with this the Ascension of our blessed Lord: 'And it came to pass, while he blessed them, he was parted from them, and carried up into heaven.' The placing of one account side by side with the other is very instructive, and suggests many points of comparison. Elijah is translated, a chariot of fire and horses of fire are commissioned to snatch him away from the earth, and carry him to heaven; but our Lord is borne upward by his innate power; He is not translated, He ascends. He came *from* heaven, and He returns *to* heaven, as to his natural home. The wonder is, not that He should now at length *go* to heaven, but that He should so long have tarried upon earth. Calmly, majestically, He ascends, carrying with Him that body which He had redeemed from the grave. No fire-chariot is needed for Him; and why? there is nothing of earthly dross requiring to be burnt out of Him, no wondrous transformation, no last baptism of cleansing fire before He can endure to pass into the presence of his Father; but such as He was upon earth, exactly such He passes into the heavens. No shock, no whirlwind, no violent rapture in his case; for in his Ascension there is no breach of the laws of his natural life, but all is in exactest conformity with them. Surely in all this matter the comparison between the servant and the Son brings out to us the greatness indeed of both; but at the same time the transcendent superiorities of the Son, who in all things hath the pre-eminence.

In what follows after Elijah has been taken up, we may have a dim foreshadowing of the history of the Church, above all the apostolic Church after the Ascension of its Lord. Elisha, we are told, the faithful disciple, 'took the mantle of Elijah that fell from him, and smote the waters, and said, Where is the Lord God of Elijah? and when he also had smitten the waters, they parted hither and thither: and Elisha went over.' The significance of this lies in the fact that it is exactly the same miracle[1] which Elijah himself had a little while before performed. Are we not here reminded of Him who, being Himself anointed with the oil of gladness above his fellows, did yet, when He left the earth, not so leave it but that He left behind Him gifts and graces and powers with his Church, endowing it with these

[1] See ver. 8.

from on high; and so effectually endowing it, that the works which He did, his Church was able to do the same, fulfilling to the very letter that promise which He had made: 'He that believeth on me, the works that I do, he shall do also, because I go unto my Father.' These powers, these gifts, these supernatural endowments, were, so to speak, the mantle which fell from our ascending Lord, the mantle which the Church took up, with which it has arrayed itself; in right of possessing which it claims to be the inheritor of its Lord's commission; in the power which that mantle imparts, seeks ever to carry on and to complete its Lord's work, to repeat and multiply his works of grace and mercy and power in the world.

And if we, brethren, we of the Church of the latter days, have seen, like Elisha, our Master taken from our head, if a cloud has received Him out of our sight, and the day of second appearing not yet appeared, what shall be our conduct, what remains for us to do? Both narratives are abundantly instructive. Elisha wasted not his time in idle lamentations; there was but that one cry, 'My father, my father, the chariot of Israel, and the horsemen thereof!' and then he girt himself to his own work, though a work to be performed in his master's strength. And the Apostles, they stood not for long idly gazing up into heaven, watching the track of their departing Lord and the path of light that He had left; but returning to Jerusalem, 'continued with one accord in prayer and supplication,' waiting for the promise of the Father; which no sooner had they received than they became witnesses to Christ 'in Jerusalem, and in all Judæa, and in Samaria, and unto the uttermost part of the earth.' They felt, and they felt rightly, that they were not weaker through his departure, but stronger. Those words of his, 'It is expedient for you that I go away,' had been a hard saying to them at the first; but it was not long before they understood them, before they tasted of the sweet which lay concealed in their seeming bitter, before they understood that a Lord in heaven, sitting at the right hand of God, receiving there gifts *for* men, and shedding abroad those gifts *upon* men, this was better than a Saviour upon earth, limited by conditions of time and space, with a Holy Ghost not yet given, because the Son of God was not yet glorified. They understood this; and let us, my brethren, ask of God that we may understand the same,—what this, our Lord's Ascension and sitting at the right hand of God, is for us and for all believers; why Ascension Day, if it does not quite attain to the dignity and honour of the first three among the Christian festivals, Christmas Day, and Easter Day, and Whit-Sunday, is yet only a little inferior to *them*, while it transcends in the dignity and importance of the event which it commemorates every other day in our Christian calendar.

Very briefly, then, Christ's Ascension is, in the first place, the complement of his Resurrection. It was not enough that He should rise from the dead and walk this earth again. He must show that not earth, but heaven, is his home, and the centre to which He is irresistibly drawn. He must take his place as the Universal Bishop, the Bishop of all souls; no longer the Shepherd of one little flock in Judæa, but the Great Shepherd of the sheep gathered in from many flocks into an universal fold. Christ's Ascension enables you to regard Him as the King of Glory, Head over all things in the Church, and as such having received gifts for men. True, there were gifts and blessings before, but not in such largeness; they were restrained, the full fountains of grace were not yet unsealed. A few drops of blessing had sprinkled a single family, a single nation; but now as a great flood it overflowed the world. The dew was hitherto upon Gideon's fleece only, and it was dry upon all the world besides; but now there should be dew on all the ground. May it richly moisten and bedew the hearts of you all.

SERMON II.

AGRIPPA.

ACTS xxvi. 28.

Then Agrippa said unto Paul, Almost thou persuadest me to be a Christian.

ALMOST, and not quite! So near the prize, and yet missing it after all! With only one step between him and life, and that one step not taken! Surely this was a tragic doom; the whole range of Scripture does not offer us a more tragic one; for, oh! the difference between the 'almost' and the 'altogether'—a difference not less than between death and life, between all which we have most to fear, and all which we have most to desire.

Who was it that uttered these memorable words, which I take as they stand in our Version, and without entering into the question whether or not they might be capable of a somewhat different turn? It was 'King Agrippa,' as St. Luke calls him; being known as Herod Agrippa the Second in profane history. It was no good stock of which he came. He was son of another Herod Agrippa, who is branded in an earlier chapter of the Acts as the murderer of James the Apostle; and who was only defeated by the interposition of an angel in his purpose of killing Peter also; of that Herod Agrippa who perished so miserably, being smitten of God in the hour of his blasphemous pride.[1] Nor was this all. He was descended from a mightier criminal yet; he was great-grandson of that first Herod who slew all the young children at Bethlehem, trusting to include in that slaughter the royal Child, to whom the throne which he occupied as an intruder and usurper rightfully belonged. There was blood enough of God's saints and servants on that wicked Herodian race; and, to do this Herod justice, there is no desire upon his part to shed more of this precious blood, or to curry favour with the Jewish people, by delivering Paul, as his father would fain have delivered Peter, to their will. Had he been such a cruel persecutor, breathing out rage and threatenings against the followers of Christ, his story would not have contained half, no, nor a hundredth part of the warning for us which it does contain. It might hardly have touched us at all.

This Agrippa was a king—one of those little kings who were permitted to maintain a shadow of royalty within the limits of the Roman Empire. When Festus, the newly appointed Roman governor of the neighbouring province, arrived at Cæsarea, the seat of his government, it was consistent with the subordinate position

[1] Acts xii. 2-4, 23.

of Agrippa, that he, though called a king, should do homage to the superior majesty of Rome in the person of the Roman deputy, and wait upon him on his first arrival, and welcome him there. After many days, spent no doubt in feasts and ceremonies and courtly revels, and when now the interest in these began to flag, and some new excitement was needed to stimulate the jaded appetite of these hunters after pleasure, Festus chanced to mention to his royal guest that a strange Jewish prisoner—his name was Paul—had been left upon his hands by his predecessor Felix. What offence this man had commited he was quite unable to make out; nor yet why the Jews were so fiercely set against him that nothing would satisfy them but his blood. And to confuse matters more, the man had claimed to be sent to Rome, and to be tried before the Emperor himself, a right which, being a Roman citizen, could not be denied him; while yet he, Festus, was sorely perplexed what account of Paul's matters, of the crime wherewith he was charged, to send with him. In fact, the whole quarrel between the other Jews and this Paul was a mystery to him. It turned on some wretched dispute of their own superstition, on one Jesus, who certainly was dead, for a predecessor of his own, Pontius Pilate, had crucified him some thirty years before; but whom Paul, who on other points seemed reasonable enough, persisted in affirming to be alive.

The curiosity, perhaps even the interest, of Agrippa is excited. Though not a Jew by birth, he was such by education; familiar with the law and the prophets, 'expert in all customs and questions which were among the Jews.'[1] He would gladly hear the man himself. Festus readily consents. It was this probably which he had been aiming at all the while. The next day they are all assembled: Agrippa and Bernice 'with much pomp,' and Paul with his chain. But being permitted to speak for himself, he so speaks, so convincingly, with such demonstration of the truth, so pressing home upon the king the claims of Jesus of Nazareth to be the Christ, the promised king of Israel, that from Agrippa at length are wrung those memorable words, 'Almost thou persuadest me to be a Christian.'

But wherefore 'almost,' and why not altogether? How came it that he stopped short where he did, and never advanced any further? Alas! brethren, it is only too easy to answer this question. Our own hearts supply, and only too well, the answer, when they whisper to us that, under like temptations, we might only too probably have stopped short where Agrippa stopped. For suppose he had been 'altogether' persuaded. What a change in all his outward conditions of existence must have followed! what a coming-down from his pride of place! To be a Christian was not so easy a thing then

[1] Acts xxvi. 3–27.

as it is now. No more of that great pomp, no more of those obsequious crowds, no more of that royal purple, no more of those flatteries and favours which the world reserves for its own, for the great and prosperous among its own children. Then too, if the king was bound, as there is too much reason to believe, in the cords of an unholiest attachment, those cords must have been snapt asunder at once, that secret wickedness utterly put away. And other thoughts, as we can little doubt, rose up before him, even the thoughts of all the scorn and all the bitter mockery which that same world has in store for those that desert its allegiance. What would they say at Rome? What would they say at Jerusalem? What would they say in Cæsar's palace; what in the Great Sanhedrim; when it was told, as the latest and most piquant news of the day, that he, that King Agrippa, had thrown in his lot with the despised Nazarene, the crucified Galilæan? All this, we may well believe, passed swiftly through his mind; he counted the cost, and that cost seemed too much for him to pay.

Truly, dear friends, it *was* much; the only question is, whether it was *too* much. Perhaps not. Perhaps he counted amiss, and another could have counted better for him than he counted for himself. Let *us* make the experiment. Let *us*, for we can do it deliberately and dispassionately, cast up his gains first, and then his losses, and set those against these. His gains, what were they?

For a few years more he kept the glories to which he clung, he played his part of king on the world's stage, and men bowed to him the crooked hinges of the knee, and paid him lip-homage, and he sat in the chief place of honour at wearisome feasts, and was the principal figure in hollow court-ceremonials and empty pageants of state; and then the play was over, and his little day was done, and darkness and night swallowed up all, and he carried nothing away with him when he died (except indeed his sins), neither did his pomp follow him. His gains then, they were not after all so very large, and, such as they were, they did not tarry with him long.

But his losses, or rather his loss? It may not seem so much, seeing that it can be summed up in a single word, and yet that word a word of awful significance. What did he lose? He lost *himself*. Christ has demanded, 'What shall a man profit, if he gain the whole world, and lose his own soul?' Agrippa had *not* gained the whole world—only a miserable little fragment of it; and this but for a moment, for a little inch of time; but in the grasping and gaining of this he had made that terrible loss and shipwreck of which Christ speaks, had lost himself; in other words, had lost all.

But now let us contemplate the matter from another point of view. Suppose, dear brethren, he had found strength actually to do that thing which he was almost persuaded to do; suppose he had made room for the truth in his heart, had been *wholly* persuaded to become a Christian, had followed on where the Spirit would have led him, how would it have been with him then? Here, again, let us count the cost for him; let us put the sufferings of this present time over against the eternal weight of glory. The sufferings of this present time— a few years of self-denial and of toil; a few hard words and contemptuous looks from the world which he had forsaken, a few buffetings from evil men; it might have been a sharp and painful passage into life; but sweetened all by the sense of God's love, by the assurance of his favour, by the knowledge of sin forgiven, of a conscience cleansed from its guilty stains through the blood of the atonement, by the fellowship of all the best and noblest upon earth, by the hope of a glory to be revealed; and then, this brief life ended, then when the expectation of the worldling perishes, when there is nothing more for him but a fearful looking for of judgment to come, Agrippa's hope would have begun to find its fulfilment, and the gates of Paradise have been thrown open to him, and the great 'Well done' have sounded in his ears. For the purple which here he renounced, he should have been clothed for ever in the white and shining garments of immortality; for the crown which here he laid down, he should have worn a crown of life for evermore. Joy beyond joy, to see the face of God, and in and through that beatific vision to be changed from glory to glory even into his likeness, to leave behind and for ever every soil and spot and stain, all impurity and defilement; and this should have been his portion for ever. Certainly it was a mistake which he made, a miscalculation, as we all must own. It *was* a rich treasure hid in the field, on which he had stumbled unawares. It *was* a pearl of great price, which had come within his reach, and he would have been no foolish merchantman had he sold all that he had, and bought this pearl. It would have proved no sorry bargain after all.

We own, we confess as much. Standing, in regard of him, upon an eminence, where the hillocks of time do not conceal from us the mountains of eternity, nor the trivialities of this life the realities of the life eternal, as for him they did, we are all ready to admit that he left the better part, and chose the worse; even while we do not conceal from ourselves the mighty difficulties which hindered him from embracing that better. But shall we stop here, with this acknowledgment? Are not all things, and these among the rest, written for our learning? What about ourselves? Are there no Agrippas now? Thou that art hesitating in thy mind, thou also convinced of sin by the power of the Spirit, but not yet converted from sin by the same Spirit, thou that tremblest on the brink of the mighty river of

God's love, and yet darest not commit thyself boldly to its waves, art not thou exactly such another as this was? Change the name, and this tale might be told of thee. Thou art this King Agrippa; thou art the man. Thou too hast said after some searching sermon, or the earnest converse of some godly friend, or after reading some holy book which has found thee out in the deeper depths of thy soul, or after some manifest dealings of God with thee by sorrow or by joy, by mercy or by judgment, thou too hast said to this book, to this sermon, to this friend, to this joy, to this sorrow, or rather to Him who was speaking to thee through all these—'Almost thou persuadest me to be a Christian, a Christian in deed and not only in name, to accept Christ for what He is, the true Lord of my life;' and yet this 'almost' of thine, like that of the unhappy king long ago, has never ripened into a 'quite.'

And why not? It rises clear before thee, the blessedness of a life in Christ, of having the deep wound of thy spirit healed, as He only can heal it, of throwing in thy lot with saints and apostles and martyrs, and all the holy and humble men of heart that have ever lived, of working *for* God, and not against Him, for the truth and not against it, the blessedness of such a life as this rises up plainly before thee; and the emptiness, the vanity, the disappointment, the defeat, the misery, the despair which must attend any other life than this; and thou too hast almost chosen thy part, even that better part which should never be taken from thee. And why not? what has hindered? what has stood hitherto in the way of so blessed a consummation? will perhaps stand in the way unto the end? Alas! exactly that which stood in the way of King Agrippa. The bands that bound him, and bound him so closely, that he dallied indeed with life and with heaven, but made a covenant with death and with hell, they are the same that bind thee.

Perhaps, like him, thou art holden by the cords of some sinful passion. Thou canst not bring thyself to forego the sweetness of it. It seems to thee that if that were taken out of thy life, the life which remained would not be worth the living, that all the wine would be drawn, and nothing but the lees remain. Or the sin may not be sweet, the sweetness of it, if it ever had any, may have departed long ago;—but though not sweet, it may be strong, binding thee with bands which thou hast no courage to break, which thou knowest thou couldst not break without a far mightier effort than any which thou art prepared to make.

Or there may be no such single well-defined hindrance to thy yielding thyself without reserve to that God, who would have thee altogether, that He might bless thee altogether; no bosom sin, dear as a right eye, almost as much a part of thyself as a right hand, which would need to be plucked out or cut off; but rather a more vague and general reluctance to yield thy will to God's, to mortify the corrupt affections of the heart, and to come under the rules and discipline and obligations of the life in Christ, the indolence of a worldly and self-indulgent spirit, than which perhaps there is nothing more effectual to keep men from Him. Or it may be, at least in part, the fear of man which oppresses thee. What will they say, the old ungodly companions with whom thou hast walked at liberty in times past, when thou announcest to these thy intention of ordering thy life henceforward by another rule, of living the rest of thy time not to the lusts of men but to the will of God?

But be these bonds what they may, oh! believe that it is worth the while to break them, as in the strength of Christ they can be broken. These mountains of opposition, it is worth while to cry to Him, that He would make them a plain. It is *well* worth the while. A few years hence, and it will be with every one of us, as it was with King Agrippa not very long after these memorable words were uttered; and then how utterly insignificant, not merely to others but to ourselves it will be, whether we were here in high place or in low, rich or poor, talked about or obscure, whether we trod lonely paths, or were grouped in joyful households of love; whether our faces were oftener soiled with tears or drest in smiles. But for us, gathered as we then shall be within the veil, and waiting for the judgment of the great day, one thing shall have attained an awful significance, shall stand out alone, as the final question, the only surviving question of our lives, Were we *almost* Christ's or *altogether*, in other words, were we Christ's, or were we not?

Oh! sadness of all sadnesses—that 'almost,' which never ripened into 'quite'; to have stood on the brink of the great river of salvation, and yet never to have committed ourselves to its waves, to have seen the King afar off, some faint glimpses of his beauty, and yet never to have followed on to know Him more, and thus never to see Him near. Oh! sadness of all sadnesses, and guilt of all guilts! And that this may be never ours, let us pray earnestly and with something such a prayer as this: 'Fix, Lord, our wavering hearts on Thee. Strengthen our weak desires for Thee. Suffer us not to fall back from Thee, even though we would. Hedge up our way behind us, though this be with thorns. Draw us to Thyself, and having drawn, bind us by any cords to the horns of thy altar. Compel us by any discipline of love, that we be not almost, but altogether, Thine.'

SERMON III.[1]

THE WOMAN THAT WAS A SINNER.

LUKE vii. 39.

Now when the Pharisee which had bidden him saw it, he spake within himself, saying, This man, if he were a prophet, would have known who and what manner of woman this is that toucheth him: for she is a sinner.

IN that well-known passage of Scripture, of which I have just cited a single verse, we have, so to speak, the title-deeds of all such Refuges and Homes as that for which I am pleading to-day; we have the special charter by which, more than by any other, they exist. In saying this, I do not imply that if no such incident as that which is recorded here, had been related in the life of our Blessed Lord, we should be without our warrant for such efforts to rescue and redeem, for such institutions as this Home, whereby there is given to these efforts persistence and permanence. I do not say this. In every page of the Gospels we might read the assurance that such endeavours are according to the mind of Christ, that

[1] Preached on behalf of a Penitentiary.

there could be no work which would better express that mind, very few that would express it at all so well. And yet, granting all this, we may be profoundly thankful that we have the special warrant for it which this Scripture affords, that we have Christ here brought face to face with a fallen but penitent woman, and that there is written at large in this Gospel the story of the infinite pity, tenderness, and compassion with which He welcomed her back, of the strong and earnest displeasure with which He regarded those who would have built up a wall of separation between Him the Holy and her the unholy.

You are familiar with all the details of this story, for none has imprinted itself more deeply on the whole heart of Christendom; how in the days of his flesh Christ sat one day at meat in the house of a Pharisee, and how, as He sat there, there came this woman 'which was a sinner' behind Him. Of much concerning her we are ignorant; in what rank of life she had once moved, among the high places of this world or the low; whether she had fallen, tempted by another, or herself the temptress; what the exact measures of her guilt had been; only one thing about her we do know, namely, that the crown of woman's honour was no longer hers, that she was a moral outcast among her people, that in the judgment of those who were regarded as the world's most righteous members, her very touch was defilement. What would there have been for her, so esteemed by others, so esteemed by herself, but an ever deeper fall, an ever more hopeless entanglement in the miry clay; a departure ever wider and wider from all things holy and pure and good; self-scorn and self-contempt, echoes of the scorn and contempt which she everywhere met in the world; these driving her ever from bad to worse—what else but this, if the righteousness of Simon the Pharisee had indeed been the righteousness of God, if a far higher righteousness, if a love, of which he knew nothing, had not been revealed from heaven, if that righteousness and this love had not met, blended, united with one another in an indissoluble union in the person of Him, who as Jesus of Nazareth now sat at that inhospitable board?

And there were dim yearnings in that fallen one, who had drunk deeply of the world's scorn, which told her this, which told her that here was One who could and would judge her sin with all severity—and what would his forgiveness have been worth, if He had not done this; if that forgiveness had rested on a shallow estimate of her guilt?—who would hate her sin with a perfect hatred, such as none other could feel about it; but who, bating no single jot of this, could regard her, the sinner, with an infinite compassion; and, if only she desired to leave her sin behind, could give her peace for the miserable past, and the power of a holy living for the time which remained. It was for this that with an unutterable longing she longed,—not for escape from future punishment; her punishment was already present, to be what she was, separate from God, an outcast from the kingdom of holiness; and Christ was the mysterious lodestar which so mightily drew her now, because there was something which whispered to her that in Him she might find again all which she had lost, and till now must have counted that she had lost for ever.

And so, bearing down in the earnestness and intensity of her desire obstacles which at another time she might have been quite impotent to overcome, she found herself in the house of the Pharisee, at the feet of Jesus, at his feet who must be her helper, her healer, her deliverer, if such there were any for her in heaven or on earth. And now those eyes, which had once shot poisonous lightnings, shed tears enough to have quenched the unholy fires which they had kindled once; while with those tears she washed the blessed feet which had deigned to tread this guilty earth of ours; and then dried them with the hairs of her head—these once the nets with which she had sought to snare unwary souls; and the precious ointment, laid up for purposes of luxury and excess, this turning to holier uses and in the prodigalities of a new affection she poured on those same feet, beautiful to her as bringing not merely the glad tidings of good things to come, but as having thither borne Him who was Himself the glad tidings which He announced.

I need not remind you how ill the proud and cold-hearted Pharisee, in whose house this gracious scene was enacted, a scene into which angels must have delighted to look, could endure it; how impossible it was for him morally to find himself in it. Salvation was indeed come to that house, but, alas! not to him that was the master of it, as it can come to none who are the sharers in his spirit. He, a loveless keeper of the law, if indeed a keeper, had looked at that law as it was graven on stones; and, as he looked, that law, like a Medusa's head, had frozen his very heart to the utter hardness of stone. She had looked at the same law, or indeed at a law higher and holier, as it was embodied in Him who was also Love; she had seen her sin there, and the condemnation of it, the pitiless condemnation of her sin—she would not have asked anything else—but at the same time had beheld there an infinite pity, a pity at once human and divine, for her the sinner; and, as she looked, hope which had been dead revived, fountains which had been stopped flowed freely forth again, the heart of stone in her was turned into a heart of flesh, and she greatly loved (we have Christ's own word for the fact) that Lord who had first loved her; and having heard and made her own the absolving words, she went forth from that presence into peace, into the heavenly peace, as the element in which henceforth her life should move.

This little history, of which I have thus sought briefly to gather up the sum, is, as I have ventured already to call it, the charter of such an Institution as this of ours, help for which I am claiming this day. Would that my voice could reach some on whom, as it appears to me, it has especial claims. Thus, in our Christian land, and growing up under favourable influences of Christ's Church, there are not a few among us, young men and old, who in their perilous youthful years were preserved, or whom the grace and providence of God is preserving now, from the corruption which is in the world through lust, who have grown up as from their baptismal root, so that amid all the faults and follies of childhood and youth they have kept that good thing which was committed to them, and have not needed painfully to win it back with toil and tears, if indeed won back at all, in an after time. Whom shall they thank for this, that they thus walked among fires which did not kindle upon them, that their feet were preserved from snares in which so many others were miserably entangled? Shall it be themselves? Shall they say that they kept themselves from their iniquity? Woe to them, self-righteous Pharisees, and not humble saints, if they count it so! Better, perhaps, to have fallen than so to stand! Was it not God, even He who keeps the feet of his saints, who strengthens them in the hour of temptation, making for them a way of escape, was it not He who upheld them? And do they not owe Him a large and abundant thank-offering for a boon so inestimable as this, one which others would give worlds, if they had them, could they now make it their own?

But, alas! there are others, and what if some such should be here to-day, who look back with shame and inward confusion at so many blurred and blotted pages of their lives; whose wounds, wounds inflicted by themselves, have been indeed healed, healed by the mighty Healer, by the effectual operation of his grace; but who will bear the scars of these wounds even to their graves. I speak not of these scars; I inquire not with what sackcloth those who must plead guilty to this accusation have clothed themselves inwardly because of these sins; but, as far as this world reaches, I would ask them to compare their lot with the lot of those whose cause I am pleading now. Those have sinned, and you have sinned—the same sin, but the penalty how different! They eat the bitter fruit of their doings to the last morsel; they drink the bitter cup of their own shame to the uttermost drop. The crown is stricken from their brows; and even at the best, and whatever good may be in store for them still, the glory has vanished from their lives, and, so far as this life is concerned, it can never come back again. But how fares it with you? Perhaps you will extenuate (I trust you will not) your faults, will urge that they were faults of youth, and have been followed and made good by the unbroken respectabilities of later age. But these unhappy ones, are they not also for the most part young? few but those who have a little experience in the matter know how young when they fall, having oftentimes lost all almost before they know that they have anything to lose. And if they fall ever deeper and deeper, from one degradation to another, remember that, as far as this world and the opinion of this world reaches, there is no recovery for them. The way of return, which is at every moment so easy for the man, is from the first impossible for the woman. The man, he has but to assume the decent proprieties of living, and all the past is at once condoned and forgotten. Some will say perhaps that you were once rather wild, that you sowed your wild oats; but they will hardly esteem the worse of you; and presently, perhaps, good things cluster round you, blessings of home, of family, of domestic life, wife and children; and the sin which the world forgave you so easily, which entailed so little of shame or loss here, you often learn only too easily to forgive it to yourselves.

Let me say here, and lest I should be misunderstood on this matter, that in some sense I do not complain that the penalties imposed by the world on sins of unchastity should be heavier in the case of the woman than of the man, unequal dealing though this may seem, unequal dealing though, when driven to excess, it is. In this making of her penalty the heaviest there is an instinct of justice, though of a justice pushed by the harshness of the world so far that it reaches an injustice. There are sanctities whereof the woman has, in the moral constitution of things, been appointed the special, though not indeed the exclusive, guardian. A glorious privilege and prerogative; but one which, being despised, must entail its own corresponding punishment. If, so far from guarding, she betrays the citadel which she was set to keep, how can the penalties be other than great?

But freely granting this, I would not the less demand of every man who hears me, and whose conscience tells him that he has at all sinned after the similitude of these sinners whom it is thus sought to save, that he too has in any degree helped forward this enormous evil which defies the benevolence of the world, and has thus far defied even the charity of the Church, let it have been in years long past, in a time divided from this present time by large spaces of decent, yea of holy living, that still he be not content without making such large and visible reparation as the case requires. The partners of his guilt, those whom he solicited, or who solicited him to sin, they may have long since passed away, may have gone down into the grave by those steep stairs of infamy and scorn and shame which lead for these unhappy ones so swiftly and so inevitably there; and he shall never meet them again until that terrible day of recognitions, when the deceiver and the deceived, the tempter and the tempted, the betrayer and the betrayed, shall stand face to face before the throne and before the Judge. But others have succeeded in their room; one miserable generation following another; and here and there one of these cries faintly for help; stretches out a feeble hand, if any will grasp it, ere she sink beneath the waves, looks round, too often in vain, if there be any who will care for her soul. Surely what he owes to the other he may pay to these; and not with such an offering as costs him nothing, which he does not so much as feel; but as one who has here to do with a God who is not mocked.

On other grounds I would make my appeal to you, wives, sisters, mothers, and through you to many more in the same relationships of life, who are not gathered with us to-day. What pinnacle of dignity and honour is like to that of a matron of our land, whose children rise up and call her blessed; and the heart of whose husband safely trusts in her? Surely her estate is queenly. But He who has given to her much, who has given her that dignity, crowned her with that honour, He makes corresponding claims at her hands. You that sit the centres of a circle of happiness in your sheltered homes, your daughters, it may be, as polished corners of the temple, growing up in fearless innocence, yea, some of them growing up in the very beauty of holiness, as far removed from the slightest contamination of this sin as the sparkling drifts of the new fallen snow from any the faintest stain or soil of the earth, do not thoughts sometimes arise in your hearts? Knowing what you must know of the corruption of our fallen nature, its mournful proclivity to evil, have you never asked yourselves how it might have fared with them, if all those jealous protections with which you have fenced them round had been wanting; if, instead of moving in an atmosphere of purity, they had breathed evermore an atmosphere of corruption; if ugly examples had been ever before their eyes, foul words often in their ears; if instead of prayers, they had been familiar with curses; if home and the sanctities of home they had never known, huddled up in crowded rooms, the very conditions of which were enough to break down all womanly self-respect, if God's word and sanctifying Spirit had never been brought to bear on their spirits; nor any of those mysterious influences of 'pure religion breathing household laws,' which have encircled your beloved from the first? Are they, think you, of such different clay from others, so far exempt from that birth-sin, which, if we believe anything the Church teaches and experience sets its seal to, is the miserable heritage of us all, that because they stand before you now, the light of your eyes, the joy of your hearts, the ornament of your lives, not merely untouched by, but in the main unconscious of, all this hideous evil, think you that, therefore, they would have done the same, if all the shaping forces, the moulding influences of their lives had been such as, alas! these are for too many? It is God, and God's grace alone, which has made them to differ, which has kept them to be, as you fondly hope, honoured wives and happy mothers, only exchanging one form of purity for another, the purity of a maidenly for that of a matronly estate.

Surely you will not dare to enjoy all these benefits, to move in this rich circle of love and joy in which God has planted you, careless of all the sin and wretchedness without it and beyond; never bethinking you, when some winter-night has gathered you and your loved ones round the cheerful hearth, of that pale form, flitting beneath the dreary lamplight, wearing the cruel stones, but not harder or more cruel than the brutal men to whose brutal lusts she is a minister—a child perhaps still in years, but with everything childlike for ever departed from her; never, I say, bethinking you of her, and how there are moments when she, this child without the innocency of childhood, this exile from all earthly love, this bird without a nest, this flower uprooted, withered, and trampled on in the mire, calls to mind that she too has a Father still, and says, like the Prodigal, that she will arise and go to Him, but knows not where to turn, or how to break the fetters which bind her so fast to that sin, which she has learned to loathe, though she has not learned how to repent it. If you have done and will do nothing here, surely an ingratitude like this were enough to make God in his anger to curse your blessings, to cause evil to rise up against you—perhaps shame and dishonour in quarters from which you looked for them the least.

I ask then help from all. The Jews will not tread on any piece of paper lying by chance on the ground, because perhaps the name of God may be written upon it. It is only a perhaps for them; but it is a certainty for us—that the name of God is written on every one of these souls now lying in the mire. They bear the image and superscription, however defaced, however well nigh effaced, of the great King. Lift them from this mire. Help to retrace that image on their souls, to restore them to the treasury of God. There may be little joy on earth when one of these outcasts is gathered in; no jubilant acclamations here when the lost is found, and one that had long lain among the pots is covered with silver wings and her feathers like gold. But there is joy in heaven, joy before the angels of God, for the tears of sinners are the wine of angels, and joy in his heart, who now sits on the throne of glory, and who once, sitting in the house of Simon the Pharisee, said to a woman who had greatly sinned, and now greatly repented and greatly loved, 'Thy sins are forgiven. Go in peace.'

SERMON IV.

JOSEPH AND HIS BRETHREN.

GEN. xlv. 3.
And Joseph said unto his brethren, I am Joseph.

DURING two whole Sundays in our Christian Year the First Lessons of the day have been drawn exclusively from the history of Joseph and his brethren. This circumstance, added to the fact that there is no portion of Holy Scripture more profoundly attractive, none which takes a stronger hold on the affections of young and old, has caused that, notwithstanding the lamentable ignorance of Scripture which prevails at the present day, and the few who find time to bestow upon it any patient study, this history is, in a certain measure, familiar to us all. Yet, this notwithstanding, I am sometimes disposed to doubt whether we at all enter into and admire as we ought the wonderful wisdom and love displayed in all those dealings of Joseph with his brethren which are crowned at length by this declaration of himself to them as the brother whom they had sold into Egypt. If I do not mistake, all which has gone before, his speaking roughly to them, his accusing them as spies, his casting them into prison, his retaining one of them in harsh durance there, his refusal to see them again unless their younger brother is with them, his causing his own cup to be found hidden in Benjamin's sack, his bringing of his brothers back under heaviest accusation, his threat to detain Benjamin as his bond-slave; all this, if I do not err, presents itself to many among us as a playing with their fears, a putting of them to unnecessary pain, a certain mitigated form of revenge in which he permits himself; or if they admit not so much as this, at any rate as a dealing with no fixed purpose and moral aim. They are unable to see *why* Joseph did not make himself known to his brethren from the first; and, seeing that he must all the while have intended to forgive them, declare this forgiveness from the beginning. With what another interest would they study these chapters, if they recognized the profound counsel of love which dictates all these dealings of his; and this counsel I will now endeavour, to the best of my power, to trace.

I have a right, as I said just now, to assume the main outlines of Joseph's history to be familiar to you all. He, the Hebrew slave, by wonderful dealings of God's providence, had been called to be a Prince and a Saviour in the mightiest and most civilized kingdom which then existed upon earth. Thanks to his wise foresight there is corn in Egypt, while a famine is raging in all the neighbouring lands: and thither, by the same leading hand of God, his brethren are brought, that they may buy corn for their households. And now they stand before him who in a manner has life and death in his hands; and yet not all of them, for Benjamin, the one unguilty, is not with that guilty company; nor is his absence difficult to explain. He is now the beloved of his father Jacob, as Joseph formerly had been. The father's preference for him may awake the same envy and jealousy and ranklings of despite in his brethren's hearts which his preference for Joseph had aroused of old. This the aged patriarch feels, and perhaps with some vague misgivings that the fate of Joseph had not been altogether as reported to him, that there was some dark secret there,—and the brothers could hardly have kept their counsel so well but that he must have surmised this,— he will not expose the sole surviving son of his beloved Rachel to this long journey and to all the hazards of one kind and another which during that journey may befall them.

Joseph recognized his brethren at once, though they failed, as they bowed before the mighty vicegerent of Egypt, to recognize in him the child by them so pitilessly sold into bondage: and Joseph, we are told, 'remembered the dreams which he had dreamed of them;' how their sheaves should stand round about and make obeisance to his sheaf; how sun and moon and eleven stars should all do homage to him.[1] All at length was coming true.

Now of course it would have been very easy for him at once to have made himself known to his brethren, to have fallen on their necks, and assured them amid floods of tears of his forgiveness. But he does nothing of the kind. He has counsels of love at once deeper and wiser than would have lain in such ready and off-hand declaration of forgiveness. He has counsels of love toward them such as God has towards the children of men. His purpose in all which follows is to prove whether they are different men, or if not, to make that they should be different men, from what they were when they practised that deed of unnatural cruelty against himself. He must know whether they at all repent that old wickedness of theirs. If there is no such repentance, he must prove whether he cannot bring such about; if there is, must seek to strengthen and deepen it; seeing that the law of God's kingdom is, that only the truly penitent are capable of being truly forgiven. At once he forms his plan; which having formed, he carries out with unshrinking hand unto the end; enduring to give some present pain

---

[1] Gen. xxxvii. 7–9.

even to that beloved father, if only those blessed issues to which he looks may be reached at last. He feels that he is carrying out not his own purpose, but God's; and this gives him confidence in hazarding all, as he does hazard it, in bringing this matter to a close.

Two things were necessary here; the first, that he should have the opportunity of observing his brethren in their conduct toward their younger brother, who had now stepped into his place, and was the same favourite with his father as Joseph once had been; whether they were jealous, evil-minded toward Benjamin, as they once had been toward himself: the second, that by some severe treatment which should bear, if this might be, a more or less remote resemblance to their treatment of himself, he should prove whether he could call out from them a lively remembrance and a penitent confession of their past guilt. Out of the first purpose, although partly also to satisfy the yearnings of his own heart, he affects to misunderstand their errand, charges them with being spies, guilty therefore of death; and thus draws out from them in their own defence the information which he most desired, namely, that their father was yet alive, and that their younger brother, whose absence may have suggested the worst suspicions to Joseph's mind, was with him. Still affecting harshness, and as giving no credit to their words, he requires that the younger brother of whom they spake shall appear before him, and so make good their assertion, else he will not believe that there is any truth in them.

Meanwhile they shall all remain in confinement as men under heaviest charges. They must taste something, though it be but the smallest portion, of that anguish which they made him to taste to the full. We can very well imagine that the prison in which they were shut up, and in which for three days they were left, was not altogether unlike that dismal pit into which they had cast him. It was the same scene, although with infinite mitigations, acted over again; only with this significant change, that the parts were shifted in it; they suffering now what they had inflicted before. And thus all the past must have risen up in their memories; for indeed sins are often written as with sympathetic ink upon the tablets of the soul; they need to be held to the fire of tribulation before even the chief actor in the sin shall himself read them there. So was it now. They began to read their past sin in the light of their present anguish; and this, although Joseph, going back in part from the severity of his first announcement, has declared now that instead of nine remaining, and only one being permitted to depart, nine may go, and only one remain in ward as a pledge for the return of the others.

Already the salutary chastening is effectually working. They cannot mistake in all this the finger of God, nor fail to see that it is their own sin which is finding them out. 'They said one to another, We are verily guilty concerning our brother, in that we saw the anguish of his soul, when he besought us, and we would not hear; therefore is this distress come upon us.' What music must these words, which they spoke little guessing they were understood, have made in his ears. With what a welcome must he have welcomed this sign which showed that the twenty years' ice of their souls was breaking up at last, and that the waters of repentance were beginning to flow freely forth. No wonder that 'he turned himself about from them and wept.' But there was no weakness in those tears of his; they did not hinder him from carrying through the work which he had begun. 'He took from them Simeon, and bound him before their eyes.' If Simeon had been, as there are many reasons to conclude, the ringleader in that foul conspiracy against a brother's life, how must their sense of being in the hands of God, and entangled in his net, have been deepened when the ruler of Egypt selected him and no other for bonds, and, should they fail to return, for death. This done, he lets the others go; but as, where there is no interference with his higher purpose of good, he must fain do them good, as he cannot bear even now to withhold from them the marks of his love, he gives them provision for the way; and, not enduring to merchandise with father and brethren for bread, he causes the money which they have paid for the corn they are carrying home to be placed in their sacks.

When they come back, and report to the aged patriarch, their father, the resolution of the lord of the country, and the only condition under which they may traffic in the land, or recover their brother there left in bonds, he breaks out into passionate lamentations, exclaiming with words truer than he knows, but the literal truth of which must have cut them to the heart: 'Me have ye bereaved of my children;' nor will he hear of an imperilling of his youngest and best beloved for the doubtful advantages held out to him in return. Thus for a while; but in the end the stern necessities of the case overcome his resolution. They shall go, and they shall carry Benjamin with them.

I will not repeat in detail incidents which are familiar to us all. This time their reception is at first more gracious than it was before. Simeon is brought forth to them. They eat and drink in the house, and in the very presence of the mighty ruler of Egypt. Strange, mysterious it must have seemed to them when he set them each and all in the order of their birthright. How could he have known this? what higher hand is working here? And then, when sending to each his portion he sends to Benjamin a portion five times larger than to any other, there is a purpose even in this. Will they be jealous of him, as they were jealous of Joseph once, of the favour which his father showed him, and of the coat of many colours which he made for him? Happily no signs of such a jealousy appear. And now they have taken their leave, and have departed homeward; yet not so, but that they carry with them, although they little guess it, that which shall presently bring them within his danger once more, and enable him, in the last and sharpest trial of all, to make proof whether their spirit now is another than that which it once had been.

Their bearing when Joseph's divining cup is at length found in Benjamin's sack is decisive of this. They rend their clothes, and prepare at once to return to the city. Had they been the same men which they had been two-and-twenty years before, this discovery would have filled them with no such anguish and despair; nay, they might rather have been well pleased without crime of theirs to be rid of that younger brother who had stepped into Joseph's place in their father's love; nor would they have taken more seriously to heart that aged father's agony at the loss of this son, than they took the same to heart on that other occasion, when they spake with icy indifference words which must have stabbed him to the very soul.[1] Had they been the men they once had

[1] Gen. xxxvii. 32.

been they would have separated, as was so easy to do, their own lot from their brother's; disengaged their fortunes from his; left him behind them to the doom which, by a mean act of ingratitude and theft (for so it must have seemed to them), he had so justly deserved. Joseph's steward, who is in his master's confidence, suggests this to them; it is afterwards suggested by Joseph himself.[1] How easily they might have satisfied their consciences, adopting such a course! They had promised, indeed, to bring Benjamin safely back; but they had never undertaken to defend him, as it was plain they could not defend him, from the consequences of his own sin.

But there is no disposition on their part to disconnect their fortunes from his, to make selfish conditions of safety for themselves. Nay, they accept his offence as their own, his iniquity as the iniquity of them all. One fate, one lot for all; or, if a better doom for any, let that be for him. Great as his fault has been, deep as the danger and disgrace into which Benjamin has brought them, they will not desert him, and by this desertion obtain, as is plain they may do, a selfish deliverance for themselves.

Their trial reaches its crisis when Joseph announces to them that Benjamin shall remain his bondsman, but that they all are free to return home. Judah is the

[1] Gen. xliv. 10–17.

spokesman in reply, and by just right; for while the matter concerns them all, it concerns him the most. He has become surety to their father for the safe return of the lad,[1] and he does not shrink from the uttermost which that suretyship may involve. Rejecting Joseph's suggestion, he makes, in the nobleness of self-offering love, another proposition. Stepping nearer in the passionate earnestness of the moment, he speaks boldly out, yet not at the same time forgetting for an instant with whom he speaks, that it is with Egypt's lord. This speech of Judah's has hardly obtained the admiration which it deserves. It is a noble model of the eloquence which sometimes visits men not eloquent by nature, when a great occasion has loosed their tongues. Briefly recapitulating what had passed since first he and his brethren came to Egypt, he puts back the temptation with which Joseph has tempted him and his brethren. Without Benjamin he will not return home. The life of his father is bound up with the life of the lad; only let the lad return with his brethren, and Judah will remain, a bondsman in his stead.

This was enough for Joseph; this was all he wanted. Brethren that could thus speak and act were not the same that had sat down in Dothan to eat bread, while he, their brother, was lying in the pit; they were not the same that had brought his raiment dipped in blood

[1] Gen. xliii. 9.

to their father, saying, 'This have we found: know now if it be thy son's coat or no.' There was nothing to hinder him now from revealing himself to them; from exclaiming, 'I am Joseph;' from falling and weeping upon their necks, in token that all the past was forgotten and forgiven, blotted out of his remembrance for ever.

I have thought good to dwell in some detail on these dealings of Joseph with his brethren, both on their own account, and also because they are, to so great an extent, the very pattern of God's dealings with men. Joseph was to his brethren in God's place, acted throughout under a divine guidance; and as he with them, so God oftentimes with us. He sees us careless, too lightly forgiving ourselves our old sins; and then, by trial and adversity and pain, brings those sins to our remembrance, causes them to find us out, and at length extracts from us a confession, 'We are verily guilty.' And then, when tribulation has done its blessed work, He is as ready to confirm his love to us as ever was Joseph to confirm his love to his brethren; nay, many times readier; for He with whom we have to do is God, and not man; He is One of whom Joseph was but a weak type and figure; every man's brother, greatly sinned against by all, rejected of his brethren, but exalted by God to the right hand of power; yet in this, his high estate, not forgetting his brethren, having compassion upon them, being merciful to their sins; pleading with them, but pleading in love; wounding, but wounding that He may heal; punishing, but only that He may bring them to confess their guilt, their offences against Him; and, this done, making Himself strange to them no more, but revealing to them the depths of that love which all the while He felt, but which only when this end was attained He was able to declare.

SERMON V.

BEARING ONE ANOTHER'S BURDENS.

GAL. vi. 2.

Bear ye one another's burdens, and so fulfil the law of Christ.

In one sense, and that the highest sense of all, Christ is Himself the only bearer of our burdens, or of the burdens of our brethren. He is the only bearer of the burden of our sins. He took that burden upon Him at his Incarnation; He bore it, and so bore it through a life of perfect obedience to the will of his heavenly Father, that He for ever bore it away when He finished his sacrifice of expiation and propitiation on the Cross. The bearing of this burden none other shared with Him, and, it is evident, none other could share; for even He, mighty as He was, upheld in his human nature by a divine personality, seemed in the garden of Gethsemane to stagger for an instant under that tremendous burden. He trod the winepress alone, and of the 'people there was none with Him.'

So too when we contemplate, not the world's sin, but the world's woe, the burden of its sorrow and anguish, there is a sense in which He bare this, as no other has borne, nor could have borne it, fulfilling the words of the prophet, 'Surely He hath borne our griefs, and carried our sorrows.' The remains of selfishness which are in every other man, which the regeneration itself does not in this life wholly abolish, cause that all others escape in great part the burdens of sorrow and anguish which He continually bore. In no other man has there existed a perfect love, and thus in no other a perfect sympathy with all the joys, and so too no less with all the sorrows of our race; not to say that the limited horizon of every other man's vision prevents him from taking in more than a very smallest portion of these joys and these sorrows; even as he is able most faintly and most inadequately to realize even that little portion which he does take in. Of all men that ever lived, Christ, and Christ alone, stood, so to speak, at the central point of humanity. Around Him stretched the huge circumference of human woe; while from every point of that dread circumference, along all the lines which converged and met in Him, the voices of human pain and suffering travelled and found sympathetic echoes in his heart; along all the lines the throbs of human anguish passed, and wrung that heart, as though each several grief had been his own. That heart was large enough to take them all in, to embrace in itself all the sorrowful that was not also the sinful, which any child of

Adam has at any time felt. The loneliness, the abandonment, the defeated hope, the despised love, the unfulfilled yearning, the torture of suspense, the suffering of the body, the aching of the spirit, He knew and understood them all. No cup of pain which had been lifted to any mortal lip, but that He tasted the bitterness of it; no depth of agony into which any human spirit had gone down, but that the plummet line of his love sounded it as well. This it was to be every man's brother, and as incarnate Love to have assumed the nature of every man.

But I can imagine some who listen to these words of mine here saying in their hearts, 'If it be indeed thus, if love opens the door to so many sorrows which else might have been shut out, if the more we have the mind of Christ, the more we shall feel the sorrows of other people, surely it is rashly and unwisely done to seek any large measure of that likeness to Him, of that love which brings these results in its train. Is not a prudent isolation of ourselves, a shutting up of ourselves within ourselves, rather to be chosen, by which we may hope to escape all this?'

Brethren, no. The way of self-isolation, in other words, of selfishness, may present itself as the more excellent way; and yet we act not less blindly than guiltily when we choose it, and this for many reasons. Let me mention some.

In the first place then, this same selfishness, this same isolation of ourselves which shuts us up against the sorrows of others, shuts us up also against their joys. If the one fountain is sealed, so will also be the other. He who will not weep with them that weep, neither shall he rejoice with them that rejoice; and thus there are sealed to him the sources of some of the purest and truest delights which the heart of man can entertain, namely, the pleasure which we derive from the happiness of others.

But then, further, it is a course as blind as it is sinful, because all experience proves that the man who lays his account to live an easy, pleasurable life by knowing nothing, by refusing to know anything, of the cares, troubles, and distresses of others, is never able to carry out this scheme of his to a successful end. In strange ways, strange, that is, as they appear to us, he is sure to be baffled and defeated in this his guilty dream of a life lived like that of the Epicurean gods, the life of one looking down as from a superior height on a vast weltering world of labour and sorrow and pain beneath him. In the profound words of the Christian poet, 'Care find the careless out;' and the man who has built up, at the cost of every duty, a citadel of selfish ease for himself, and made the defences strong, and set watches at every gate by which it seemed possible that any foe to his peace, any troubler of his enjoyment, might enter, that man sooner or later is doomed to discover what feeble and ineffectual barriers are all these. In an instant, at a single bound, the enemy whom he thought to exclude overleaps and stands within the defences which he had reared at such cost and pains, or enters at some unguarded postern gate; and he who would not have so much as a crumpled sere leaf beneath him, finds himself tossing on a bed of pain, sharp set with piercing thorns; he who would not stretch out a little finger to lighten the burden of another, groans under the intolerable weight of his own.

And why is this sure to be the issue of all such selfish schemes? Because God reigneth; because He will have it so; because He sets Himself against the man who sets himself against the law of Christ, the law of love. 'Bear ye one another's burdens, and so fulfil the law of Christ:' these are the words of the Holy Ghost by the mouth of the Apostle Paul; and he who resolves not to bear any part of the burdens of his fellows, resolves not to fulfil the law of Christ; and if God is Judge, if his face is against them that do evil, what can come of any such walking counter to his will, but a curse, and not a blessing, for him who has resolved so to order his life?

But, further, bear ye the burden of one another's sins. In one sense, as we have seen already, Christ only can do this. And yet, while this in the highest sense of all is supremely true, there is a secondary and inferior sense in which *we* may bear this burden for one another. Did not St. Paul, for example, bear the burden of the sins of these same Galatians, when, because they had suffered themselves to be seduced by false teachers into ways of self-righteousness and spiritual pride, he needed to begin again from the beginning the whole work of their conversion, and to bring them back by painful steps to Christ and his Cross once more?[1] And we, brethren, what must we do, if we would bear this burden for one another? We must not soon be provoked; we must be patient toward all men; seeking, if they be overtaken with a fault, to restore them in the spirit of meekness; not hugely angry at any discomfort or loss or annoyance which their faults may entail, while we remember how often and in how far greater things we have provoked the patience of God; accepting therefore this which their sin may lay upon us as part of that burden which sinners dwelling among sinners must expect to bear. So too we bear the burden of other men's sins when we take trouble, endure toil and pain and loss in seeking their restoration; when, at however remote a distance from our Lord, we too follow them into the wilderness, that so, it may be, we may find, and having found may bring them home again.

And as it is a duty to bear the burden of one

[1] Gal. iv. 19.

another's sin, so is it also to bear that of one another's weakness, of those infirmities which are not sin, although only sinful creatures would be subject to them. 'Support the weak,' this was the solemn exhortation which this same Apostle uttered on a very solemn occasion.[1] You, for example, may be strong in faith; you may be able to lay firm hold on the promises of God in Christ, to cast the anchor of your faith sure and steadfast within the veil; yet do not therefore despise, be not impatient with him who at every step is ready to halt, who is full of doubts and fears, who cleaves to his Saviour with a weak trembling faith, which hardly knows itself to be faith at all. You may think another full of needless scruples; and perhaps he is so, and God may have given to you the gift of discerning things that differ, which He has withholden from him; or you may count him narrow-minded, and wanting in any large views of the truth; yet bear with him, bear the burden which these scruples, this narrow-mindedness of his may impose upon you, as possibly a most useful discipline, which God through this same brother has provided for you.

But, lastly, bear the burden of one another's sorrows. What simple, and yet what sublime, words are those, which in the Gospel story we so often read concerning the Lord, 'He had compassion on them.' Let the same mind be in you that was also in Christ Jesus. How

[1] Acts xx. 35.

often quite another mind is ours! There are too many who might be likened,—one of our old divines, in his quaint way, has likened them,—to the hedgehog, which, wrapping itself up in a ball, keeps all its soft warm wool within and for itself; has nothing but sharp prickly spines which it presents to them that are without. And indeed is not this, my brethren, the exact image of the selfish man? And when I speak of him, think not that I mean some monster of cruelty and hardness of heart, against whom the very world cries shame. Oh, no! the selfish man whom the word of God denounces is simply the man who will bear no burden which he can evade, who will enter into no sorrow from which he can decently escape. He may be polite, he may be courteous, he may be good-humoured; he may be even good-natured, where good-nature will entail on him no serious trouble; he may shed tears over fancied sorrows, yes and over real ones, where they are specially adapted to move the imagination and the feelings; but for all this, self is the centre round which his whole life and being revolves. To keep things painful at a distance from himself, to draw round himself a charmed circle, into which these shall be unable to intrude, this is the aim and object, I may say the ambition, of his life.

Brethren, if this be our ambition, if, so far as means and opportunities will admit, it is our study to effect this for ourselves, I do not say but that we may partially and for a time succeed; we may be cursed with that which is the greatest curse of all, namely, success in evil doing. But of this be sure, that our gain here will be indeed our loss; so to save our life will be to lose it; and a day will arrive when we shall discover this. Oh, miserable retrospect for him who himself lies at length on a bed of languishing; to whose own lips is put at last that cup of anguish which, with careless eye, he has seen go round to a thousand others; who is submitted now to those stern realities of pain and all the terrible teaching which they bring with them; oh, miserable retrospect for him who, looking back through a long vista of years, cannot now but remember that, living in a kingdom of love, he has yet shut his heart to all love; a sinner, whose only hope was in the mercy of God, he has yet failed to shew that mercy to men which he so greatly needed that God should shew to him. With wealth perhaps and leisure and talents, and golden opportunities (now, alas! for ever fled), he has yet smoothed no pillows, wiped away no tears, sustained no weak, bound up no broken, borne no burdens, poured the oil and wine of consolation into no wounded hearts; and now the mercy which he has not shewn, how can he hope that it will be shewn to him?

Wouldst thou escape such a miserable looking back, such a miserable looking forward? There is only one way to do this. Cast thyself boldly forth into the kingdom of love. See what burdens of thy brethren thou canst there come under. Fear not these burdens, that they shall crush thee to earth; so strange is their operation that, rather, they shall be wings lifting thee to heaven. Fear not that they shall take all joy out of thy life; so far from this, thou shalt enjoy thy life, as never thou enjoyedst it before. They who have tried declare no less, declare too that this bearing of the burdens of others makes our own burden far lighter when it comes. And if at any time thou faintest, or growest weary, or shrinkest from this, there is one sure secret of strength, and it is this: Consider Christ; consider Him who, in the days of his flesh, bore the burden of the world's woe; who on his cross bore the burden of the world's sin; who is the bearer of thy burden now, else thou wouldst not be in the kingdom of grace; who must be the bearer of thy burden at the last, else thou wilt never be in the kingdom of glory; and who will only so bear it upon one condition, that thou doest the things which He has said, that thou fulfillest his law, even the royal law of love. This if thou wilt not do, as thou wilt have rejected love, the kingdom of love, and He who is the Prince in that kingdom, will reject thee. Thou must bear thy burden for thyself; and thou who knowest the secrets of thine own heart and thine own life, wilt best be able to judge whether that burden will or will not be too heavy for thee to bear.

SERMON VI.

THE LOVE OF MONEY.

1 TIM. vi. 10.
The love of money is the root of all evil.

IF we in our sermons speak seldom,—and it must be owned that we do speak seldom,—of the sin of covetousness; if only at rare intervals and in mincing terms we bid you, and in you ourselves, to take heed of it, there is assuredly no warrant for any such reticence in Scripture. There, as in these words of St. Paul, 'The love of money is the root of all evil,' or in those other of Christ our Lord, 'Take heed and beware of covetousness,' we are warned with all plainness of speech against it; even as we are again and again reminded there of other sins and further dangers which this sin draws after it; as, for instance, how 'they that will be rich fall into temptation and a snare, and into many foolish and hurtful lusts, which drown men in destruction and perdition.'[1] Nor is the warning of Scripture by earnest words only, but by terrible examples no less. What a dread procession

[1] 1 Tim. vi. 9.

of souls, which losing heaven, very often did not win that earth for which they were content to lose it, is made there to pass before us: Achan, who thought to enrich himself with that wedge of gold and that Babylonian garment; and for whom that wedge of gold served but as it were to cleave his soul asunder, while that Babylonian garment proved to him no better than a winding sheet:[1] and Gehazi, with the two talents of silver and the five changes of raiment, which he obtained by a lie from Naaman, but did not make account of the garment which he should never change, of that robe of leprosy which should cling to him and to his children for ever:[2] and Balaam, who loved the wages of unrighteousness, but who took no gain of money, though he had made shipwreck of all that he might take it:[3] and there, too, is the betrayer, who purchased 'the field of blood' with the reward of iniquity, being himself the first to handsell that field with his own.[4]

These, as you well know, are but a few of the beacon lights which in Scripture have been kindled to warn us from the rocks and quicksands on which so many have perished; while yet with so many of these warnings there, the like are not, as I urged just now, very often heard in our pulpits. How shall we account for this? Is it that our people are assumed not to be so much

[1] Josh. vii. 21-25.
[2] 2 Kings v. 22-27.
[3] Num. xxiv. 11.
[4] Acts i. 18.

exposed to temptations from this quarter as were others in the days of old? or do we take for granted that, however exposed to these temptations, you have all in the main victoriously overcome them? Or do we hold our peace from quite an opposite cause? Is it that we despair of making head against a sin which has grown so mighty, and thus count it our safest course not to display our helplessness by making impotent war against it? or, saddest of all, can it be that we, who should denounce this sin, are tongue-tied, as knowing that if any could read *our* hearts, and all which is working there, it would be only too easy to retort on us, 'Physician, heal thyself; thou, who denouncest this sin, art thou not thyself holden as fast as any other in the cords of it?' I presume not to offer the explanation; but the fact can scarcely be disputed, that, taking into account the immense prominence which in so many of the affairs of life questions about money assume, the infinite temptations to which men are exposed through their eagerness to get, their unwillingness to part with this, they are very inadequately guarded against these temptations by any monitions which from our lips they receive. Let me for once at least break through this habit of silence, and address to you some words on this matter.

'The love of money,' says the Apostle, 'is the root of all evil;' not that all evils have, but that all may have, their root therein. To say that all evils do actually spring from this root would be an exaggeration, and more than the truth. Pride and lust, the world and the flesh, are both roots of evil quite as really as the love of money; and have their own evil offshoots as well. But there is no evil, St. Paul would say, which may not spring from this root. Take a rapid glance of a few of these, to which it certainly gives birth.

And first, what a root it is of idolatry; or rather it is not so much a root of this, as itself this idolatry—'covetousness, which is idolatry.'[1] This sounds a hard saying, but it is one which can justify itself. For what is the essence of idolatry? Is it not a serving and loving of the creature more than the Creator; a giving to the lower what was due only to the higher, what was due only to Him who is the highest of all? Men are idolaters when, instead of saying, 'The Lord is my Shepherd, I shall not want,' they say, 'I have much goods laid up for many years;' or, to translate this into modern language, 'I have an ample rent-roll,' or 'I have a large balance with my banker, and therefore I shall not want.' Will any, looking at his own heart, deny that worldly goods in possession or in imagination do mightily tempt men to lean on them; and, if an earnest watch be not kept, are very powerful to draw away the heart from a simple and childlike trust in Him who clothes the lily, and feeds the young ravens which

[1] Col. iii. 5.

call upon Him; and who will much more clothe and feed his own children that are better than these?

And as this love of money disturbs the relations of men to God, drawing off to some meaner object affections due to Him, so it mingles continually an element of strife and division in the relations of men with one another. How often it has caused brethren in the faith, yea, and brethren in blood, to fall out; been, as it were, an apple of discord among those most bound to love one another. Such it would inevitably have proved for Abraham and Lot, if the nobleness of the character of the royal-hearted patriarch had not made this impossible. But all are not followers of Abraham here.[1] Which of us has not known families that dwelt once in love and peace together, and might have done so to the end if it had not been for the dividing of the inheritance? But out of this what of secret rancours, of open quarrels, has sprung; of strangeness, and often of much more than strangeness, put between brethren; of enmities which seem as though they would never cease, which are transmitted from one generation to another, a miserable heirloom of strife and debate.

Again, what a root of unrighteousness, of untruthful dealing between man and man, of unfair advantage taken of the simple and the ignorant, of falsehood, fraud, and chicane, does the love of money continually show itself

[1] Gen. xiii. 7-9.

to be! *How* fruitful a root of these only that last day will declare, when all 'the hidden things of dishonesty' shall not be hidden any more. But even now, when so much is covered and concealed which shall then be laid bare, we can see enough and too much of the rank harvest of robbery and wrong which grows from this single bitter root; I mean of robbery and wrong as in God's sight; for very much in these things, stopping short of that whereof the laws of men take cognizance, and bringing men under no pains and penalties of human tribunals, is not the less hateful in the eyes of Him who is a God of righteousness and truth; and, though the laws of man may have no power to touch it, is not the less contrary to *their* profession, who, as children of light, are bound to walk in the light, and to have no fellowship with ought which will not endure to be made manifest by the light.

And then—for time would fail me if I dwelt at large on all the mischiefs that spring from this, which even the heathen poet could style 'the accursed hunger of gold'—what treading on the poor; what thrusting of them on unwholesome and dangerous occupations, with no due precautions taken for their health and safety; what shutting up of the bowels of compassion from the Lazarus lying at the gate; what wicked thoughts finding room in men's hearts, secret wishes for the death of those who stand between them and some coveted possession, have all their origin here; that I speak not of other and worse sins than these, when the wicked thought embodies itself in the wicked act, 'the treason of the murdering in the bed,' with all other those monstrous deeds written in the annals of crime, whereof certainly our age has been as fruitful as any which went before it.

But such outbreaks of strange wickedness, you say, lie out of the range of the temptations to which you are exposed; there is no need to warn you against such. Be it so; though indeed there is no sin which another has ever committed, but that we, under like temptations and provocations, might commit the same. Let this however pass, and let us concern ourselves only with those other less enormous outcomings of the evil springing from this root; and bear with me a little longer, while I suggest some considerations which may help us to take up arms against a sin which, like some pernicious ivy, is ever seeking to twine itself round our hearts, till it strangle all the nobler life of our spirits.

Consider then, first, how powerless riches are against some of the worst calamities of our present life; how many of the sorrows which search men out the closest, which most drink up the spirit, these are utterly impotent to avert or to cure. Men think of them as of a strong tower, to which they can always resort, and whither no enemy can follow; and therefore they are so eager to heap them up; or, if this is out of hope, count those happy who are able to do so. But take an instance of their impotence; the case (not so uncommon) of one suffering intense and persistent bodily pain. Ask a man in a fit of the stone, or a victim of cancer, what his riches are worth to him; why, if he had the wealth of the Indies ten times told, he would exchange it all for ease of body, and a little remission of anguish.

But why speak of bodily anguish? There is an anguish yet harder to bear, the anguish of the man whom the arrows of the Almighty, for they are his arrows, have pierced; who has learned what sin is, but has stopped short with the experience of the Psalmist, 'Day and night thy hand was heavy upon me; my moisture is turned into the drought of summer,'[1] and never learned that there is also an atonement. What profits it such a one that all the world is for him, so long as he feels and knows that God is against him? He may cover and conceal his spirit's hurt with purple and gold; but it does not the less gnaw inwardly, and take all joy and gladness from his life.

Then, too, how often we see a man comparatively desolate in the midst of the largest worldly abundance. He has loved, and the beloved, the desire of his eyes, has been early taken from him, and he runs his long-widowed course, and paces his empty halls alone, nourishing a secret grief, which all that this world gives is

[1] Ps. xxxii. 4.

quite unavailing to assuage. Or with large possessions he goes childless, and, like another Abraham, sees some stranger, some 'Eliezer of Damascus,'[1] on whom shall devolve the inheritance of many generations, or the newer wealth for which he himself has toiled and carked and cared. Or, sadder still, he has children, but riotous, unruly, disobedient, who plainly are only waiting for the moment when he shall be in his grave to scatter with usurers, with jockeys, with gamblers, with harlots, all which he has so carefully watched over, or so painfully gotten together. Surely, as the wise king said long ago, 'this also is vanity.'

These considerations may do something; but take now another and a more effectual remedy against this sin. Let a greater love expel a less, a nobler affection supersede a meaner. Consider often the great things for which you were made, the unsearchable riches of which you have been made partakers in Christ; for covetousness, the desire of having, and of having ever more and more, sin as it is, is yet the degeneration of something which is not a sin. Man was made for the infinite; with infinite longings, infinite cravings and desires. He was intended to find the satisfaction of all these longings, all these desires in God; ordained by the primal law of his creation to hunger and thirst for God, and to be satisfied only with Him. But averting

---

[1] Gen. xv. 2.

himself from God, the hunger and the thirst still remain, the sense of emptiness, the yearning after something which he has not got, the desire of having, of filling that immense void within him; and now, because he has refused to fill it with the fulness of God, he seeks to fill it with the fulness of the creature, with ever more and more of this; which however, do what he will, leaves him dissatisfied and yearning still; for none are truly filled save those whom God satisfies, and satisfies with Himself.

But finally, the habit of largely and liberally setting apart from our income to the service of God and the necessities of our poorer brethren is a great remedy against covetousness. I do not mean lazy and promiscuous almsgiving, with no pains taken to know whether our gifts are well bestowed—emptying our seed-corn out of the sack's mouth, instead of carefully scattering it with the hand; for this can do nothing except harm. But I mean a wise and deliberate dedication of a portion *to* God, of that which *all* came *from* God. Nor need I urge that this portion, if it is really to help us in mortifying the corrupt affection of covetousness, must not be a very small and niggard one. It must not be that paltry residue which, in most cases, is all that is likely to remain, if indeed anything at all will remain, after every taste, every fancy, every desire of our hearts has been gratified. I say not how much it should be. That tithe of our income which some have laid down as an absolute rule, supplies at all events a most useful test, suggests a proportion to which an approximation might be most fitly made. But whether more than this, as it might very well be with many, or less than this, as it might be with others, or this exact amount, of one thing I feel sadly sure, namely, that any dedication of a portion of our income which at all approached to this, would be ten times, twenty times more than that amount which a large number of those calling themselves Christian, and believing that they are fulfilling their duties as such, actually dedicate at the present. Our charities, the offerings which we offer to God, too often cost us nothing, and therefore, as a consequence, they profit us nothing; they help us little or not at all in the way to heaven; nay, rather, in their littleness serve only as an acknowledgment that we recognize a duty which yet we are refusing to fulfil. Some perhaps will say, Better then to withhold this little, if it shall thus prove a witness against us. They may say this; but they cannot in their hearts believe that any true help is here. That help can only lie in so multiplying this little that it may witness not against us but for us; that, like the alms of Cornelius, which, as you will remember, were 'much alms,' it may come up for a memorial before God.[1]

[1] Acts x. 2, 4.

SERMON VII.[1]

THE ARMOUR OF GOD.

EPHESIANS vi. 13.

Wherefore take unto you the whole armour of God, that ye may be able to withstand in the evil day, and having done all, to stand.

THERE is but one kind of armour, brethren, which, after all is done, proves of any value, and that is the 'armour of God.' It is only through putting on of this that a man, or a nation, is able to do that which the Apostle desires here that the Ephesians may be enabled to do—namely, 'to withstand in the evil day, and having done all, to stand.' It greatly behoves, therefore, all those who believe that such an evil day may come, that in one shape or another it must come, earnestly to inquire what this 'armour of God' is, and whether they have indeed put it on; seeing that without this preparation all other preparations will avail nothing. 'A horse is counted but a vain thing to save a man;' we may make up our breaches, and fortify our strongholds; we may enlist in the service of war the latest discoveries

---

[1] Preached to the Queen's Westminster Rifle Volunteers.

of science; we may build navies which shall sweep the seas; the tramp of armed battalions may wake unwonted echoes in the streets of our cities; and yet for all this, in one way or another, there will be found a fatal weakness in all our preparations; there will be flaws and rifts in our armour; our battlements will be taken away, for they are not the Lord's; wisdom and counsel will perish from the wise and prudent; yes, too, and courage from the brave; and this at the very moment when such are needed the most; and God will plainly shew that all those who put their trust in an arm of flesh, and, if only that arm seem sufficiently strong, care little for any other support, are trusting in a vain thing, which cannot profit nor deliver.

But some may perhaps ask here, What is this 'armour of God,' of which you speak? We can understand this man or that being bidden, in his own single and personal conflict with sin and Satan and with evil men who are his instruments, to take such armour, and array himself with it. It is a figure, yet one sufficiently intelligible. We can understand also why it should be promised to him who obeys this bidding, to this soldier of God, to him and to him only, that he shall stand in the evil day of temptation and trial. But a people or nation, how can *they* put this armour on? What does this language mean in respect of them? The conflicts which they wage, they are with outward, not inward foes—with flesh and blood, not with spiritual wickednesses. With what 'armour of God' can they be clothed? And granting that such is in their reach, how can this affect the issue of conflicts which are not spiritual but carnal; which are fought not with spiritual adversaries, but with flesh and blood, with men of like passions with themselves?

Questions such as these might easily rise up, not in the hearts of some, but of many. Let me endeavour to answer them. And first, I am bold to affirm there is 'armour of God' for a nation as well as for an individual. Travel in your thoughts to the verse next following my text, and you will find the several pieces of this armour enumerated, the breastplate of righteousness, or, as it is elsewhere, of faith and love, the girdle of truth, and so on with the rest. But these, righteousness, faith, love, and truth, these are not matters which pertain to us merely in our single separate relation to God; but also most closely in our relation with our brethren. They affect all the conduct of man to man, all the relations of class with class, of high with low, and poor with rich; of the husband with the wife, of the child with the parent, of the master with the servant, of the buyer with the seller; of the wise with the simple; of the ruler with the ruled; of the Queen with her subjects; of the subjects with their Queen. There is not one of these relations, in which, and in the fulfilment of the duties flowing out of that relation, we may not put on this 'armour of God,' if we will—that is, there is not one of them in which we may not act lovingly, truthfully, faithfully, righteously with our brethren; battling against and overcoming the ever-recurring temptations to act otherwise; shewing our faith by our works; shewing that we fear and honour God by just and true and affectionate dealing with our neighbour.

But this being so, what I would say is, that when such a dealing is the predominant rule and law of a nation's life, when, despite the multitude of exceptions which may be found, still in the main class deals justly with class, when the rich do not tread upon the poor, nor the poor grudge against the rich; when children do not rise up against their parents, but reverence, fear, and obey them; when, with fewest exceptions, husbands and wives keep faithfully the vow and promise between them made; when uprightness and honesty is the general law in the dealings between buyer and seller; when truth is spoken between man and man; when God's law and God's word is acknowledged as the ultimate test and touchstone by which everything is to be judged, and to which everything is to be brought; I say, when it is thus with a nation, we may venture to affirm of it, despite of all the sins, all the evils which it may harbour in its bosom, that it has put on the armour of God; and judging of the future by the past, we augur that it will stand in whatever evil days may arrive.

And if it be further asked, *why* a nation may be therefore expected to stand; the answer is not merely that God will be with it, that God will bless it, may correct, but, in the midst of his loving corrections, will not give it over to death. This is indeed true; but over and above this we may see and trace very plainly *how* and in what several ways the elements of goodness in it will be also in themselves elements of strength and power and endurance. The absence of class jealousies, of envies, emulations, heart-burnings, and with this the knitting of the heart of the whole nation as the heart of one man, what an element of strength is this in the day of trial. Again, mutual confidence between man and man, what another source of strength is here; while the want of this confidence, mutual distrust, the uncertainty whether the man you lean on the most may not prove a traitor or a coward, is as rottenness in the bones. Then, too, where the home is holy, where the sacred fire burns purely on the domestic hearth, there is a beauty, a sanctity, a blessedness about the life of the family, which is felt by thousands and tens of thousands to be worth living for, and worth dying for—which arms the patriot heart of the father, the husband, and the brother, to do and dare all in the defence of homes which are so precious; yet only so precious because they are so pure. In these and in a thousand ways more, which time will not permit me to recount, this '*armour of God*,' being, as it is, armour of righteousness and truth, of purity and love, approves itself as that which makes a nation strong, which nerves its arm, and establishes its heart, which enables it 'to withstand in the evil day, and having done all, to stand.'

If then it should appear likely that such an evil day is now approaching for us, if perilous times are perhaps at hand, times that will try to the uttermost men and nations, how momentous a question is this which presents itself to us? Have we, as a people, taken to ourselves the armour of God? Are we as a nation clothed with it, with that armour of light, that panoply of God, which is at once a light and a defence, a sun and a shield? I look round me, and, blessed be God, I see many tokens for good, that it is even so; much to give us assurance that, notwithstanding the overflowings of ungodliness which sometimes make us afraid, the heart of this people is sound; much for which to thank God and take courage; though mingled, as I am bound to say, with very much which might most justly fill us with misgiving and alarm.

Bear with me, suffer me while I touch very rapidly on one or two of these tokens and auguries that are not for good, but for evil. Thus I spoke just now of the sanctity of the family life, the strength which there is in a people who are under the influence of 'pure religion breathing household laws.' But the sense of this sanctity, reverence for that most sacred bond of all, the bond of marriage, from which all family life proceeds, must have waxed feeble, must have well-nigh disappeared among large numbers of our people, before ever the nation could have been startled from its dream of self-righteousness by such miserable revelations as those which our Divorce Courts within the last few years have afforded. Or look at our streets by night, yea, and oftentimes by day, full of the unhappy and fallen members of one sex, who minister to the coarsest lusts and most sensual appetites of the other. What a yawning gulf of perdition opens here before our eyes, and one into which many a young man has cast all that was best and noblest and purest, yes, and I am bold to affirm, all that was bravest in his heart—therein to be swallowed up for ever.

Again, are we, one is sometimes tempted to ask, as just and upright a people as once we were? We are richer, more prosperous, more flourishing now than our fathers were. We conduct business on a grander scale; we smile at the petty returns which satisfied them. But are we a more righteous or as righteous a people as they in their narrower line of things were of old? Is there the same truth, the same fairness, the same mercantile honour which once existed among us? Are there not some tokens which seem to say no? How shall we explain those laws which it has been found necessary to pass, hindering one manufacturer from assuming, that is, from forging, the name and trade-mark of another? how shall we explain the almost recognized rule, so that scarcely any shame attends the avowal of it, that lying measures, which proclaim themselves one thing, and are quite another, lengths which are not nearly so long, and breadths which are not at all so broad, as they proclaim themselves to be, may be passed off and palmed on the unsuspecting buyer, and that with no brand of fraud on the seller?

Other questions, alas! like these, I might ask. I might count up *our* sins; sins of the clergy, quite as easily as sins of the laity; or sins of the higher, rather than sins of the middle, class; but let these suffice. In these, and in such as these, are the rifts of our armour. Here are the true perils of the nation; here, in these sins of ours, is that which justifies any misgivings about the future which we may entertain. For if righteousness exalteth a nation, so also sin is not merely, in the words of the Wise King, a reproach to any people, but undermining, as it does, the moral strength, eating out the moral heart, of a people, leaves it in the end naked and defenceless—a Samson with all the outward shows, it may be, of his strength remaining, but with his locks shorn, and that strength indeed gone from him;

though perhaps he will not discover this till the Philistine is upon him, and he goes forth thinking to rid himself of his adversary as in the days of old.

My brethren, whom we have rejoiced to welcome within these walls to-day, you will not, I am sure, account one word which has been spoken as intended to depreciate the importance of that mighty national movement in which you have borne and are bearing your part. So far from slighting or underrating it, I accept it as itself one of our most hopeful tokens for good; while the absence of any such national muster in perilous times like these would be indeed one of the worst among those tokens of ill which I spoke of just now, a most disastrous augury for the future, a fatal evidence that indolence, and effeminacy, and the love of ease, and the unwillingness to endure hardness, or to affront danger, had gone far to take away the man's heart from us, and left us poor and contemptible in our own eyes and in the eyes of the world, a people without valour, or, in other words, without worth—a carcase around which, according to the immutable laws of God's government in this world, the eagles would presently be gathered together, as round their appointed prey.

But in this national gathering you and your fellows throughout the land have declared that it is not thus, that there are things dearer to Englishmen than their ease and their safety, their comforts and their luxuries, their buying and selling and getting gain—that this land of ours, which has known how to reconcile the prerogatives of an ancient line of kings with the liberties of an advancing people, this land so full of the monuments of past greatness, and the pledges of greatness to come, this citadel of freedom, this bulwark of the pure and reformed faith of Christ throughout the world, is a land dear to them, dearer, if need be, than the life itself. They have avouched their conviction, that of all this glory and this greatness, these blessings of pure religion and temperate freedom, this marvellous heirloom of the past, we, this living generation of Englishmen, account ourselves in God's sight the guardians and the trustees. For indeed these treasures are not ours—not ours, that is, in fee, that we may do with them what we will—lose, squander, dissipate them, if we are so minded; but as we received them from our fathers, so we are bound, by moral obligations the most binding, to hand them down unimpaired, undiminished, to our children; nay, more than this, to bequeath them if possible a richer, more glorious inheritance than we received them.

For this is the true law of a noble nation's life. To each generation which in succession at once *is*, and *represents* it, there is granted the use and enjoyment of priceless blessings—blessings of law, of liberty, of order, of national dignity and glory—blessings which that generation did not win, but which others in ages past won for them—obtained for them oftentimes at the price of costliest sacrifices, by patience and endurance, by toil and tears, not seldom upon battle-fields, in dungeons, and on scaffolds. But with the use and enjoyment of these blessings is also committed to each generation in turn the guardianship of them; that this which they have inherited suffer no loss, no diminution, while passing through their hands. Nay, this does not satisfy the just claims which may be made upon them. They are bound, as others before them were, to improve what they have received, to perfect what may be still lacking therein, to repair the injuries and decays which the lapse of years may have wrought, to redress the wrongs and supply the shortcomings which the course of time may reveal; to make their special contributions, as others before them have made theirs, to the glory, the honour, the well-being, the moral no less than material prosperity of that dear land which has given them birth, and to which they owe a mightier debt than they can hope ever perfectly to repay.

And indeed, brethren, I know not what shame, what ignominy, what scorn, would not rightly be *their* portion, what curses of an indignant posterity would not justly light upon *their* heads, who should betray a trust so solemn and so awful as this is—the generation which should not merely fail in leaving better what they found good, in leaving greater what they found

G

already great—but of whom in the records of all after time it should be written, that they found England great, and that they left her small; that they found her crowned and sceptred, a royal land, and that they left her servile and sitting in the dust; that they found her the inviolate island of the free, and left her polluted and profaned with the hostile foot of the stranger; that they found her the chiefest and the first, and that they left her among the lowest and the last.

Friends and fellow-countrymen, it is because you are resolved to do your part to avert even the remote possibility of such a dishonour, such a reproach from yourselves, that you are in arms this day. Men of peace, addicted to the arts of peace, habituated to the pursuits of peace, it is your dearest wish to live peaceable lives, and, as I would fain trust, to lead those lives in all godly quietness. You know something of the hateful guilt of war; that every needless unrighteous war, undertaken out of greed, or pride, or ambition, or love of glory, or lust of dominion, or desire of revenge, is a crime huger, darker, deeper, entailing a more frightful guilt upon its authors, than any other in the dread catalogue of human crimes; being as it is a crime on a far more gigantic scale than any other can possibly be. But in this guilt, at any rate, you feel that you can never be entangled. You, by your very constitution, are rooted to your native soil. No ambitious warrior or statesman, even if he should desire it, could ever use you as instruments of wrong-doing towards others, of aggression upon the rights of your neighbours. It is with your feet planted upon this English land, amid the graves of your fathers, among your own hearths and homes, that you, if ever the occasion should arise, will give proof of your manhood; not as men inflicting wrong upon others, but only as those who would avert intolerable wrong from us and from yourselves.

But knowing this guilt of theirs, the wasters and destroyers of the earth, first-born of Cain with the mark of the arch-murderer on their foreheads, their guilt, who to the Moloch of their ambition or their pride offer hecatombs of the lives of men, you know also that there is another guilt, which we dare not affirm to be less; even the guilt of those who might have guarded, who might have defended against the mightiest and worst of these, the blessings which God had given them; but who, out of sloth, or cowardice, or vain confidence, or slight esteem which they set upon his gifts, cared not to do so, suffered these to be wrested out of their hands, made shameful shipwreck, not of their own blessings alone, but of the blessings of countless generations to come. He who will have his gifts esteemed at a just price from time to time puts a nation to the proof. He says to it, not in so many words, but in a language which cannot be mistaken, At what rate do you prize these blessings of mine, whereof you make your boast? What sacrifices will you undergo to keep them? Do you count them worth contending for? Do you count them, if need be, worth dying for? By your presence here, clad not in the garments of peace, but in the livery of war, you have avouched that you do. Your answer to this question is, Yes ; being the same answer which you are prepared to give, as now in this house of peace and prayer, with no danger in sight, so also amid sterner scenes, and mingling this Yes of yours, not as now with the rolling peals of the organ, but with the dreadful voices, the thunder-music of war.

But words of boasting, words which might seem however remotely to savour of boasting, become not us, nor this house of God, nor yet the occasion which has brought us together. Rather let us devoutly seek of Him the consecration of those arms which we have not willingly, but only by the strong constraint of duty, assumed. Let us humble ourselves every one in his sight, confessing our own sins and our people's; wherein consists the true danger which threatens us, the danger which draws all other dangers in its train, and which makes them dangers indeed; seeking pardon for those sins through the precious blood of Christ. And when we have thus cleansed our bosoms from the miserable burden of unconfessed, unrepented, unforsaken, and therefore, unforgiven sin, let us seek to put on the whole armour of God; to put it on ourselves, to help others to put it on; armour of righteousness, armour of purity, armour of truth and love; and then, God being our helper, whatever evil day may come, whatever foes may assail, be they spiritual wickednesses alone, or enemies of flesh and blood as well, we may humbly yet confidently hope that we shall be able to withstand in that evil day, and having done all, to stand.

SERMON VIII.

THE THORN IN THE FLESH.

2 Cor. xii. 7-9.

And lest I should be exalted above measure through the abundance of the revelations, there was given to me a thorn in the flesh, the messenger of Satan to buffet me, lest I should be exalted above measure. For this thing I besought the Lord thrice, that it might depart from me. And he said unto me, My grace is sufficient for thee: for my strength is made perfect in weakness. Most gladly therefore will I rather glory in my infirmities, that the power of Christ may rest upon me.

An eminent father of the Western Church has loved to remark, and has indeed remarked several times over, on the exceeding preciousness which the grace of humility must possess in the sight of God, and on the evidence of this which we have in the fact that St. Paul was submitted to such a discipline as is here recorded, that he might the more surely retain it. The same illustrious teacher has not failed further to remind us, and to remind us often, of the fatal ease with which this excellent grace may be lost, when a Paul himself could be in peril of losing it; and, seizing that which above all is the distinctive warning in this passage conveyed, he earnestly bids us to note the strange and unexpected quarters from which this grace is assailed, so that the very gifts and favours bestowed by God upon his own may minister food and fuel to their pride, may exalt them in their own conceit, and cause them to let go a grace, which in this resembles charity, that if a man have it not, then having everything else, but not having this, he is nothing and worse than nothing in the sight of God. Lessons of such vast importance to us all being wrapt up in this Scripture, it may be worth our while to examine it a little closer.

St. Paul has just told the Corinthians of favours strange, rare, wonderful, which had been vouchsafed to him, of 'a man in Christ,' by all acknowledged to be himself, who was 'caught up to the third heaven,' 'into Paradise,' who had there heard words more wonderful than could find utterance again in any dialect of earth, as indeed must be the case with any words of heaven; who had there glimpses of glory vouchsafed him such as have been seldom permitted to any child of man while yet abiding in this tenement of clay. But, he goes on to say, 'Lest I should be exalted above measure,' lifted up too high 'through the abundance of the revelations,' lest he should grow dizzy even at the recollection of those heavenly heights on which he walked for a while, and losing his head should stumble and fall, 'there was given to me,' God of his grace provided for him, 'a thorn in the flesh, the messenger of Satan to buffet me,' lest, as he twice repeats it, 'I should be exalted above measure,' and that which was meant to be his wealth should turn out not wealth, but poverty, not a lifting up, but the most terrible casting down of all.

Now what exactly this 'thorn in the flesh,' of which the Apostle speaks, was, the Corinthians knew very well; but *we* do not know, and we never shall know with any certainty; nor does it greatly concern us that we should know. Only of this we may be quite sure, from the purpose with which it was sent, and the language in which it is spoken of, that it was something to vex and annoy him, to humble and keep him low, some effectual antidote to spiritual pride. Various conjectures have been hazarded about it. Among these perhaps the following commend themselves the most. First, it has been suggested by some that this 'thorn in the flesh' was some temptation—a 'messenger of Satan' in this sense. There is perhaps nothing which more effectually humbles a man who has been walking upon spiritual heights, who has been brought into near and high communion with God, drunk deeply of the river of his pleasures, than afterwards to find that, despite of all this, he is still obvious to the meanest and lowest temptations of the flesh or of the spirit; that Satan can still suggest to him envious thoughts, or impure thoughts, or proud thoughts; and that, however he may have fancied that he had left all these very far behind, there is that in him which is only too ready to respond to these suggestions of the enemy. Some temptation in one of these kinds or another that 'thorn in the flesh' may very possibly have been.

Others, again, have proposed quite a different explanation: that by this we are to understand some man, such a one, for example, as Alexander the coppersmith, of whom St. Paul himself bears witness that he greatly withstood his words;[1] some man who, even in the matter of human gifts, was immeasurably St. Paul's inferior, and who yet was permitted to resist him, to sow tares where he had sown good seed, and in various ways to hinder and traverse and undo his work. This, too, has something to recommend it. Doubtless it would have been an infinite humiliation that he, with his lofty and noble purposes, his wondrous endowments, natural and supernatural, should yet have been effectually withstood by so mean and vulgar an adversary as this.

Once more: there have been others who have seen in this 'thorn in the flesh' some bodily ailment, cramping the Apostle's energies, crippling his powers, entailing the necessity of painful remedies, and never suffering him to forget that body of humiliation which he carried about. An infirmity such as this, feelingly reminding

[1] 2 Tim. iv. 14, 15.

him what he was, would have been a school excellently fitted for the learning of humility and the unlearning of pride. It has been the school in which many of God's saints have learned *their* lesson of humility, and may have been that in which St. Paul was learning his. There is a passage in his Epistle to the Galatians (I refer to iv. 13, 14) where he speaks of an 'infirmity of the flesh,' called by him presently after his temptation in his flesh, which may very well have been something of the kind.

But whatever this 'thorn' may have been, it was a thing so painful, so unwelcome to flesh and blood, so hard to be borne, it seemed, in the Apostle's mind, so serious a hindrance to his apostolic labours, perhaps also to his own growth and progress in the spiritual life, that he thrice besought the Lord that it might be taken from him. By this 'thrice' we may understand that he set forth three several seasons, these at some interval from one another, and made it at each of these the special purport and object of his prayer that this which so vexed, harassed, and annoyed him might depart from him, might not be permitted to buffet him any more.

What was the Lord's answer to his servant? Did He allow his petition? In one sense He did; in another He did not. In a higher and more real sense He did; in a lower and apparent sense He did not. His request in the letter of it He did not grant, but in the spirit of it He did. He did not grant it in the letter. The precise boon which St. Paul asked, namely, that this 'thorn in the flesh' might be taken from him, this was withheld. But why had he asked this? That his work for Christ might not be hindered; that the higher life of his own soul and spirit might not endure any wrong. And the Lord's answer is to this effect, that these objects will be best attained by suffering this to continue which he so longed to see removed. So will he learn evermore to walk humbly with his God; so will he be saved from that worm of pride which is ever threatening, like a canker, to eat into and to destroy the fairest fruits of the Spirit. In the sense of his own weakness he will learn the secret of God's strength; empty of self, he will be filled with the fulness of God. 'Thou askest that this should depart, but I have a better boon for thee. This shall remain, but strength and grace shall be added to thee sufficient to bear it; and thus thou shalt learn lessons of humility, of faith, of patience, of hope, which thou wouldst have never learned if I had too lightly answered thy prayer.' But was not this to answer it indeed? and does not the Apostle feel that it was so when he goes on to declare, 'Most gladly therefore will I rather glory in my infirmities, that the power of Christ may rest upon me'?

Having given this rapid oversight of the Scripture

before us, have I not a right, O my friends, to affirm that it is full of comfort and instruction for all? Say not in your hearts that this case of St. Paul's was an exceptional case; that we cannot be caught up into the third heaven; that there is no danger lest we should be exalted by an abundance of revelations; that the record, therefore, of these passages in the inner life of St. Paul may be curious and interesting, but can have no close or near application to ourselves. I am sure that in our humbler spheres they have a very real application; and this I will endeavour to show.

If, then, we look round us, and examine closely the lot and condition of men, even of those who seem the most signally favoured of fortune, if, I say, we nearly regard this, we may in almost every case perceive that their happiness is not complete and full-orbed; or, if it appear so for an instant, like the moon at the full, presently the shadows begin to encroach, and there is a rim of dark, larger or smaller, on the orb of every man's joy. Something is wanting to every man, even to him whom the world counts the most favoured of all. He is rich, but a stranger, it may be, shall inherit all that he has. He is famous in the world, but has no joy at his domestic hearth. A noble career opens to him, but health fails, and he must renounce it. Fortune seems to give everything, but yet in a strange irony withholds the one thing, which would make all the rest to have any true value. There is the whole row of cyphers, but the one figure before them, which would make them express anything, is wanting.

Thus fares it even with the favoured few; but this, of course, is still more observable with the many who have no such rare and exceptional gifts; everywhere something absent whose presence would have been desired—something present which would have been wished away; some good thing withheld, or some sad thing added to every man's condition; in other words, some 'thorn in the flesh.' It is sometimes evident to all the world; in other cases the world knows nothing about it, and none except the sufferer himself knows; but he knows only too well the irritation, the annoyance, the disquietude, 'the fever and the fret' of which it is a constant source to him. How easy it is to grow impatient, angry, under a discipline such as this—perhaps at first to ask that it might be removed, that it might depart; to ask this once and again; and then if, as it seems, we are not heard, to fret and murmur against the Lord. Very often a man is the more irritated and provoked by it because there is nothing grand, or romantic, or heroic about it. It is some very commonplace, very ordinary annoyance, with no striking features about it, nothing to present the sufferer as a martyr in the eyes of a pitying and admiring world. Had there been such, then we might have borne it with some sort of patience;

but such ordinary, ignoble trials, rather humbling than exalting us in the sight of men, these are hardly to be endured with any meekness of patience.

Alas! brethren, we do not know that such messengers as these to humble us are a part, and a most important part, of the discipline of our lives. It takes very little to puff up these vain hearts of ours. Let only a little success, a little prosperity, attend us, and we are ready to burn incense to our own drag, to count that our own wisdom and our own prudence have procured it; little as we have in which to exalt ourselves, still to exalt ourselves above measure in that little. Let the world bestow on us a few of its flatteries and its smiles, and we are ready to throw in our lot with it; to say in our hearts, 'This is our rest,' and not so much as to desire any better rest than it can give. How would it fare with us if the poison of this pride and this worldliness wrought in us without an antidote? The 'thorn in the flesh,' that is the appointed means to keep us low, to prevent us from yielding ourselves to the world altogether, its votaries and its victims, to remind us that we are sinners, living among sinners, and can only look in this present time for a sinner's doom. That is it which shall bring us in right earnest to a throne of grace, and make us to desire a better country and a heavenly.

Or apply this which has been just said to the more directly spiritual life of men. There is perhaps nothing which so much disappoints the young and earnest Christian as the slow progress which he makes in holiness. There is nothing which surprises, which oftentimes casts him down, so much as this, after he has tasted that the Lord is gracious, and known something in his heart of hearts of the power and sweetness of God's word, to discover that he is still exposed to temptations of the lowest, the meanest, the most grovelling kind—temptations to little exhibitions of vanity, to little untruthfulnesses in word or deed, to petty acts of selfishness, to impure thoughts and unholy imaginations. He had hoped that he was to travel on from strength to strength, from one height of Christian attainment to another and a higher height, without let or hindrance. He, too, having been in his third heaven, counts that he shall never come down from it, that he shall walk ever as on the battlements of heaven; or at any rate does not expect that henceforth he shall be liable to the every-day vulgar temptations which he sees to be besetting so many round him. Soon, however, he learns his mistake. The way of holiness is a much more tedious way than he had supposed. He is much farther off from the goal than he had imagined. Many humiliations, many painful discoveries of indwelling corruption are still before him. The Canaanite will dwell in the land, and does not give place for one, no, nor yet for many defeats.

You remember what the Lord said concerning the

literal Canaanites, when the children of Israel were about to take possession of the land:—' I will not drive them out from before thee in one year, lest the beasts of the field multiply against thee. By little and little I will drive them out from before thee, until thou be increased and inherit the land.' Is there not a profound teaching for us here, whether it was directly intended or no? If the Lord had driven out the Canaanite at once, and before Israel was strong enough and many enough to occupy the whole country, the beasts of the field would have multiplied upon them. What are these 'beasts' but the pride, the elation, the lifting up of the heart, the vain confidence in self, the forgetfulness of God, which would grow upon the Christian, if, in the days of his novitiate, and at the first onset, he were allowed to carry all before him, to take the whole land of his future inheritance in possession at once? His very victories would be more disastrous than defeat, would themselves be his ruin. Therefore to him also is given, given of a gracious God, 'the thorn in the flesh,' one, or it may be many temptations constantly recurring; and, even while of God's grace he is able to overcome them, humbling him not the less by the mere fact that he has to take up arms and earnestly contend with foes so mean and so unworthy. Oftentimes he passes through the whole experience of St. Paul; he prays that this messenger of Satan may depart from him; but learns that God has provided some better thing for him; that better thing being, not release *from* temptation, but victory *in* and *over* temptation. We in our sloth and indolence may not esteem it better; but we have God's assurance that it is.

Therefore, brethren beloved, if there be any among you vexed, hindered, hampered by obstacles, annoyances, infirmities, temptations, besetting your outward or your inward life, murmur not for these, neither say how much better it would be for you if only these would depart; on the contrary, they are very probably an essential part of that appointed training for heaven under which your God sees it good that you should pass. And if you have besought Him to free you from the vexation of these, and He has not done so, do not therefore conclude that He has not heard. He has heard, though He may not have granted, and this in very faithfulness and love; for to his enemies He often grants their petitions in anger, while to his friends He refuses them in love. So fared it with his servant Paul, when *he* besought Him thrice that the thorn in the flesh might depart from him. To him the Lord made answer, 'My grace is sufficient for thee: for my strength is made perfect in weakness.' Shall not the answer which satisfied an Apostle also satisfy thee? Wilt not thou also accept it for what it is, an answer of grace, and learn to say with him 'Most gladly therefore will I glory in my infirmities, that the power of Christ may rest upon me'?

SERMON IX.

ISAIAH'S VISION.[1]

ISAIAH vi. 1–3.

In the year that king Uzziah died I saw also the Lord sitting upon a throne, high and lifted up, and his train filled the temple. Above it stood the seraphims: each one had six wings; with twain he covered his face, and with twain he covered his feet, and with twain he did fly. And one cried unto another, and said, Holy, holy, holy, is the LORD of hosts: the whole earth is full of his glory.

WE have here in this wondrous vision the proper inauguration of the great Evangelical prophet to his future work; and one which, in its essential features, resembles very closely the inauguration which other eminent servants of God, alike under the Old Covenant and under the New, obtained; which Moses obtained, when God spake to him out of the burning bush,[2] and he at the first 'hid his face, for he was afraid to look upon God;' which Jeremiah obtained, when God put forth his hand, and touched his mouth, making *him* a meet ambassador of his, who had said just before, 'Ah, Lord God! behold, I cannot speak: for I am a child;'[3] the same inaugura-

---

[1] Preached on Trinity Sunday.   [2] Exod. iii. 6.   [3] Jer. i. 6–9

tion which Paul obtained, when suddenly on the way to Damascus a light shone round him, blinding him outwardly, that it might illumine him inwardly; casting him down once, that it might lift him up for ever; the same inauguration which many more, need I mention Joshua,[1] and Gideon,[2] and Ezekiel,[3] and Peter,[4] obtained; for God's messengers go not until they are sent, and presume not to deliver a message which they have not received directly from the Sender. We have here then, I say, the prophet's legitimation to the solemn work of his life; and we shall miss the meaning of this sublime Scripture, its significance for him, its significance for ourselves, unless we contemplate it as such.

And first, he gives the date of the vision. What meaning may there sometimes be in a thing which seems so simple as a date! What significance, what solemnity may it sometimes have, as surely it has here: 'In the year that King Uzziah died I saw the Lord.' What would he say here but this, 'In the year when the crowned monarch of the earth went down into the dust and darkness of the tomb, and all the pomp and pageantry which had surrounded him for a little while dissolved and disappeared, I saw another King, even the King immortal, sitting upon his throne, which is for ever and ever'? How simply and yet how grandly are

---

[1] Josh. i. 1.   [2] Judg. vi. 12-24.
[3] Ezek. i. 2. [4] Luke v. 4-10.

earth and heaven here brought together, and the fleeting phantoms of one set over against the abiding realities of the other.

But if his throne is in heaven, the skirts of his glory reach even to the earth: 'his train filled the temple;' and around and above that throne stood—for they were in the presence of their King—the seraphims in burning row, themselves a living circle of light; while yet before the more awful brightness of Him who sat upon the throne they veiled their faces and veiled their feet; for 'He charges his angels with folly, and the heavens are not pure in his sight.' And of these, 'one cried unto another' in the great antiphon of heaven, 'and said, Holy, holy, holy is the Lord of hosts: the whole earth is full of his glory.'

I should call you to note at any time, above all I must call you to note at this, the glimpse afforded here to the Church of the elder dispensation of that great crowning mystery which the Church of the newer dispensation throughout all the world is celebrating to-day. In this trisagion, in this thrice repeated Holy, we have, it is true, no more than a glimpse of the mystery; even as in the Old Testament more is nowhere vouchsafed. More, in all likelihood, the Church could not then, nor until it had been thoroughly educated into a confession of the unity of the Godhead, with safety have received; while yet it was a precious confirmation of the faith, when, in a later day, this mystery was fully made known, to discover that the rudiments of it had been laid long before in Scripture, that first and last were there bound together, the full unfolded flower of the New Testament shut up in the bud and blossom of the Old, that known to God were all his works from the beginning.

Such were the sights and such the sounds which were vouchsafed in the visions of God to the prophet's eye and ear. It needed but a touch of the divine hand to transport him out of himself, and to show him these. And the same sights and sounds of another, of a higher and a purer, world, they are round about us still. We cannot see them, we cannot hear them, clothed as we are in this 'muddy vesture of decay'; but not the less they are very nigh to us, everywhere round us; we moving up and down with only a thin veil separating us from them—and this a veil, which when the hand of God shall draw aside, we too shall see the King upon his throne; and shall see Him, either to rejoice in the light of his countenance for ever, or to perish utterly in the intolerable brightness of his presence.

But the prophet—what is the first impression which this glorious vision makes upon him? Is it joy? Is it rapturous delight? Is he bathed as in the bliss of Deity? In the presence of God, in nearness to Him, does he find the fulness of joy? Strange to say, it is altogether otherwise with him. His first cry is not of exultation and delight, but rather of consternation and dismay, 'Woe is me! for I am undone.' Strange, I said, and yet, if we meditate a little, not strange at all. For how can the near revelation of the Holy God be aught else but terrible to unholy man; revealing, as it does, the dread antagonism between them; the war, which must be a war to the death, unless some way of reconciliation shall be found? And when I say unholy man, think not that I mean this man or that, who may have wrought more evil, drunk up iniquity with a greater greediness, than his fellows; but I include every man, the relatively holiest no less than the relatively unholiest man that is born of woman, every child of this fallen race. For all alike, this nearness to God, this standing in his immediate presence, seeing, as it were, his face, this, except under conditions of which presently we shall speak, breeds the extremity of anguish and of fear; and though God is life and the one fountain of life, it is, as it were, a very message of death. Even the heathen, as more than one legend in their mythology declares, could apprehend something of this truth. If Jupiter comes to Semele arrayed in the glories of deity, she perishes, consumed to ashes in a brightness which is more than mortality can bear. So, too, it must have fared with Moses, if to him, still clothed in flesh and blood, that over-bold request of his, 'Shew me thy glory,' had been conceded; if it had not been answered to him, 'Thou canst not see my face; for there shall no man see me, and live.'[1] 'We shall perish, for we have seen the Lord of Hosts,' was the ever-recurring cry of those saints of old; and even such is the voice of the prophet here, ' Woe is me! for I am undone; because I am a man of unclean lips, and I dwell in the midst of a people of unclean lips: for mine eyes have seen the King, the Lord of hosts.' He who uttered this cry was one, as none can doubt, who had kept himself from his iniquity, holding the mystery of the faith in a pure conscience; and yet in that terrible light he saw and avouched himself as a man undone, saw stains in himself which he had not imagined before, discovered impurities which he had not dreamt of before, saw his own sin and his people's sin,—for he did not feel that he could separate himself from this, acting and reacting as these had done upon one another,—till that mighty cry of anguish was wrung from him. Those lips of his, with which he should have taken part in that heavenly hymn, they were 'unclean lips'; and if those were unclean, then that truth in the inward parts, that absolute cleanness of heart which God requires, he must have felt to be wanting too.

Ah, dear brethren, we who are bearers to you of the word of Christ are often sadly perplexed that we find it so hard, so well-nigh impossible, to bring down

---

[1] Exod. xxxiii. 18-20.

some whom we address from the high places of their self-conceit; to lead them to take that first step in the Christian life which consists in giving glory to God and taking shame to ourselves. But have we not the explanation here? They have never even remotely known that which Isaiah knew when he stood in that awful presence; never seen themselves in that terrible light which laid open and manifest to him all of himself which hitherto had been hidden even to himself. Remaining wilfully at a guilty distance, it has been never given to them to behold even the remotest skirts of the glory of Him on whom the Seraphim wait, to catch the faintest echoes of that angelic song, that 'Holy, holy, holy,' which fills the temple of heaven and of earth; and so they live on, their hearts unconsecrated to Him, their lips uncircumcised by Him; perfectly satisfied with themselves, and never dreaming that one thing, that one thing which is everything, is lacking to them still.

But yet, it may be asked, how should we wish it otherwise; how should we wish that light, which makes all things manifest, to make manifest to them these hidden things of themselves, seeing that such manifestations, such revelations of God's holiness, call out in them whose unholiness is thus laid bare, voices of dismay and fear, like that of the prophet, 'Woe is me! I am undone'? It may be asked, Do we wish to call out such a voice of anguish in any among you? Yes, dear friends, even so.

It is exactly this cry which we *would* call forth from every one among you who has not uttered it already; for indeed so to be undone is not to be undone, but rather to be made for ever; and what we fear for some is, not that they may utter this 'undone,' but that they may never utter it—never, that is, until it be too late. Awful moment (I will not deny it), dreadful moment (who will affirm otherwise?), is that for any human soul, when God first reveals Himself to it as the all-holy; reveals his law, which has been broken a thousand times, as the righteous and eternal law of the moral universe; when we know that the evil which we have done never can be undone; when we do not as yet know that it can be done away; forgiven, and forgiven on the ground which alone satisfies the deepest cravings of the conscience—namely, because the penalty of it has been already paid. A moment *that* in the spiritual history of a man, when death seems rather to be chosen than life, the burden of discovered sin as one greater than the soul can bear; and yet that moment with all its dreadfulness is a passage, in some sense the only passage, into a true life.

And such the prophet found it; for hear what follows; hear God's answer to this cry of his, and then judge whether this does not justify me in saying that so to be undone as he was, is not to be undone, but rather to be made for ever. 'Then flew one of the seraphims unto me, having a live coal in his hand, which he had taken with the tongs from off the altar: and he laid it upon my mouth, and said, Lo, this hath touched thy lips; and thine iniquity is taken away, and thy sin purged.'

Observe, I beseech you, the manner in which sin, I mean the *guilt* of sin, is here, as evermore in Holy Scripture, spoken of as taken away by a free act of God, an act of His in which man is passive; in which he has, so to speak, to stand still and see the salvation of the Lord; an act to which he can contribute nothing, save indeed only that divinely awakened hunger of the soul after the benefit which we call faith. It is quite another thing with the *power* of sin. In the subduing of the power of sin we must be fellow-workers with God; all the faculties of our renewed nature will need to be strained to the uttermost. So, too, it is quite another thing with the *stain* of sin: this, to be effaced, will demand the fuller's soap and the refiner's fire; the patient toil, it may be the many tears, of him who would indeed have this stain effaced from his soul. But, in the matter of getting rid of the *guilt* of sin, we have nothing to do but to stand still and see the work of our God. This is the universal language of Scripture, and with nothing less than this will the heart of men be content. When Joshua the high-priest (the passage, let me say, constitutes a most instructive real parallel to the present) stands before the Lord 'clothed with filthy garments,' the word of grace which goes forth concerning him, 'Take away the filthy garments from him,' is in its essence identical with this; the interpretation of that symbolic act following close upon the act itself—'Behold, I have caused thine iniquity to pass from thee.'[1] It is this which in Scripture the saints of God, who feel themselves sinners too, crave after; such an act of taking away as shall be wholly God's, and which, as being such, shall be perfect—'Purge me with hyssop, and I shall be clean: wash me, and I shall be whiter than snow.'[2] It is this which the soul, rejoicing in its deliverance from the condemnation of sin, avouches that it has received: 'As far as the east is from the west, so far hath he removed our transgressions from us;' or again, 'Thou wilt cast all their sins into the depths of the sea.'[3]

Still and evermore this forgiveness is represented to us in Scripture as purely the work of God;—of God through Christ, as we have learned in that clearer dispensation under which we live; though it was not a whit less truly through Christ in the times of that elder covenant. Indeed He that sat on the throne, whose train filled the temple, before whom the Seraphim veiled their faces, whom they hymned with alternate song, He at whose bidding one of these flaming fires touched the

[1] Zech. iii. 1-5.   [2] Ps. li. 7.   [3] Mic. vii. 19.

prophet's lips with the coal from the altar, He was Himself no other than the Son in his pre-existent glory, in the form of God, in that form of God which was from eternity his own. This we might safely have concluded from the analogy of other Scripture; for all the appearances of God in the Old Testament are appearances of the Son, anticipations of his Incarnation; but we do not need to argue it. We gave St. John's distinct declaration that the glory which Esaias at this time saw was the glory, not of the Father, for no man hath seen Him at any time, but that of the only begotten Son of the Father, and that Esaias, speaking these things, 'spake of him.'[1]

Let us keep, then, that distinct which the Scripture keeps distinct—deliverance from the guilt of sin, which is God's act and his only, and deliverance from the power and dominion of sin, in which we must bear our part, in which we must be fellow-workers with Him. Distinguish them, if you would have any true peace, a conscience which shall be indeed at peace with Him; distinguish, but since God has joined, see that you do not so much as attempt to divide them. Think not (it will be a vain thought) to keep the peace and the joy, while you are not following after the holiness, while you are not yielding yourselves to God, and offering yourselves to do his work and to run in the

[1] John xii., 40, 41.

way of his commandments, now that He has set you at liberty.

If you do, will not the prophet who has been leading our thoughts this day himself condemn you? Behold in him the fruit of iniquity taken away, and of sin purged. Behold the joyful readiness with which he now offers himself for the service of his God. A moment before he had cried, 'Woe is me! I am undone;' but now when the voice reaches him from the throne, 'Whom shall I send, and who will go for us?' at once he offers himself, 'Here am I; send me.' O joyful liberty of those whom Christ has made free! He stops not here to enquire whereunto the Lord would send him, to undertake what painful labour, to drink what cup of suffering, to be baptized with what baptism of blood. Be the task what it may, he is ready for it.

And you, dear friends, who have known the grace which he knew, will you not offer yourselves, if you have not offered yourselves already, for that work, whatsoever it may be, to which your Healer and your Purifier would send you? Shall there be no 'Here am I; send me,' from that lightened heart, from those cleansed lips of yours? Your mission, it may be humble, or it may be high; the adorning the doctrine of Christ in some lowliest estate, or the adorning of it in some highest, and before kings; the teaching of some little child, or the helping to cast down some huge iniquity which darkens half a world. Isaiah's mission, we know what that was; cast your eyes but to the close of the chapter, and you will see that it was from that day forth to bear to his people the saddest message and burden of woe which it could be committed to a loving heart to bear; even as there is all reason to believe, that in the end it was appointed to him to resist to the death a bloody and idolatrous king; and, if Jewish tradition may be trusted, only in the fire-chariot of an agonizing martyrdom to pass into the presence and to see for ever the face of that King immortal, of whom now this passing glimpse was vouchsafed him.

It is to humbler trials, to easier tasks, that in all likelihood He invites you; but He does invite, He does expect you to offer yourselves to these: 'Lord, what wilt thou have me to do?' And say not that this question has been asked already, and that you have received no answer to it. What, is not everything within and without you an answer to it? Within you —is there not abundance there to be done, and that He would fain see done; a work of grace begun indeed, but which needs in every direction to be deepened, strengthened, purified; a work of grace which has strangely lagged and loitered since that day when in baptism you were made a child of God, and made free of all the powers and privileges of the heavenly kingdom? And without you, in a world like ours, in such a world of woe, is there no work for Christ's volunteers, for any and for all who have a willing mind to the work? Look around you, and will you then dare to say this? What, are there no burdens that you can bear, no tears that you can staunch, no ignorance that you can scatter, no hearts which have utterly lost faith in the goodness and love of God, which you may bring back to faith in Him and in his love, by shewing what love there is in the children of God? See to it, I beseech you, that your faith be no barren acquiescence in what God has wrought for you, with an indolent resting thereupon; that your joy go forth for the gladdening of others; else, be sure, it will presently be no joy at all for yourselves; the very springs of it will soon be dried up. If God has given to you any of his peace and joy, then when He says, as presently He will say in your hearing, and meaning that you shall hear, 'Whom shall I send, and who will go for us?' see to it that Isaiah's answer be also yours, 'Here am I; send me.'

SERMON X.

SELFISHNESS.

Phil. ii. 4, 5.

Look not every man on his own things, but every man also on the things of others. Let this mind be in you, which was also in Christ Jesus.

These words contain a warning against selfishness. It is a singular fact that the *words* 'selfish' and 'selfishness' should be of comparatively recent introduction into the English language. They are little more than two hundred years old, and were quite unknown to Shakespeare and the writers of his time. They first make their appearance in the writings of some of the Puritan divines towards the middle of the seventeenth century, and were remarked on, sometimes condemned as novelties, at the time of their first employment. I say it is a singular fact that the *words* should be so new, seeing that the *thing* is so old. Selfishness, or the undue love of self, is as old as sin, is as old as the Fall, or indeed as old as the Devil. I called it just now the *undue* love of self. Perhaps I should have called it rather, the love of our *wrong self*. There is a self belonging to us, and that our true self, which it is our duty to love, as is plain from that precept of Christ, 'Thou shalt love thy neighbour *as thyself*'—seeing that in this precept the love of self is made the rule, measure, and law of our love to our brethren; which it could not be, if it were itself a condemnable thing.

But perhaps some may ask, What do I mean by the *true* self in every man, which he not merely *may*, but *ought* to love, seeing that by this he is to learn his love to his neighbour, and measure what that ought to be? I answer, that in every redeemed man there is not one self only but two, a true and a false, a nobler and a baser, a life which he is to love and to cherish, and a life, one indeed which is not so much a life as a death, which he is to mortify and to kill; and selfishness is a man's love of the wrong self in him, a pampering and cherishing of this, with a corresponding slight, neglect, and injury done to the right self, to that higher nature in him which came from God, and should return to God; and which it is the bounden duty of every faithful man to nourish, sustain, and develop in himself as in others to the uttermost.

If therefore the question were put to any one of us, Is it right to love oneself? it would be desirable before answering, to put a question to the questioner, and to ask him, What self do you mean? Do you mean that nobler life which God planted at the first in me and in every man, which, when sin had nearly extinguished, Christ revived in me again, extricated from all which was crushing it, and from which it never could have extricated itself? Do you mean that life which shall endure for ever and ever, which shall survive when this world and the fashion of this world shall all have past away? If you mean this, I answer, It is right to love this, to provide for it whatsoever will most help its growth and progress, to remove far off from it whatsoever would be its injury and bane; in all ways to cherish and make much of it. But if, on the contrary, you mean by self that meaner, baser self, which, alas! I bear about with me still, and which craves present gratification, and which in every thing makes its own interest, its own honour, its own ease, its own pleasure the foremost consideration, postponing and subordinating every other consideration to these, I answer, It is not right to love this self; for this self, the miserable result of Adam's fall, the legacy which he has bequeathed to his children, and which not one of them has repudiated as he ought, was suffered to remain in us, redeemed, regenerate men, for our exercise, that we might, in the power of the Holy Ghost, mortify, subdue, and in the end abolish it utterly; not that we might feed, pamper, and nourish it up to a fiercer activity. And when we speak of selfishness, we mean this love of our wrong self—the loving that in us which we ought to hate, our disease and not our health; and, as will necessarily follow, though we may not intend it so, a hating that in us which we ought to love; inasmuch as these are contrary one to the other, and all that is added to the one is taken from the other.

But selfishness, thus explained, may seem to include *all* sin; and so, no doubt, it does. The two words are properly, and in their ultimate grounds, exactly coextensive with one another. But while in absolute strictness of speech this is so, selfishness in our common acceptation of the word occupies a somewhat narrower domain. It expresses all those undue preferences of self, of that meaner self whereof I just spoke, which display a manifest indifference for the feelings, the interests, or the safety of others; and to the end that my subject may not lose itself in infinite space, it is of selfishness in this its common and narrower acceptation that I desire to say something before we part. Let me show, by one or two instances from Scripture, exactly what I call outcomings of selfishness, as distinguished from, though not opposed to, outbreaks of sin in the general. For example, when St. Paul and his company on their way to Rome were overtaken by that terrible tempest in the Adrian Sea, and would have perished, if the lives of all them that sailed with him had not been given to Paul, we read that the shipmen or sailors let down the boat, and were about to abandon the ship and all who were in it.[1] Here was a glaring piece of selfishness; not merely did these sailors consult only for their own safety, but they so consulted for it, as, humanly speaking, to ensure the destruction of all who sailed with them; for what faintest glimpse of hope would have remained, when all who understood the management of the ship had forsaken it? Strangely enough, that same story of St. Paul's shipwreck supplies another example of the same thing. Yet I ought not to say, strangely; for great perils are the touchstone of every man; and as they call out in nobler natures all that is noblest in them, so in meaner natures all that is meanest. When it was evident that the ship would go to pieces on the shore, 'the soldiers' counsel was to kill the prisoners,' Paul included, 'lest any of them should swim out, and escape.'[2] They thought, that is, that there might be some remote possibility of danger to themselves, that they might be held answerable, if any of the prisoners should escape (an almost impossible thing), and therefore proposed to make short work of it, to release themselves from this slightest shadow of a danger by taking the lives of these helpless prisoners committed to their charge. The pages of Scripture would afford other examples in like kind; but let these suffice.

[1] Acts xxvii. 30. [2] Acts xxvii. 42.

We need only to look around us upon that actual world in the midst of which we live, or indeed to look within us upon that interior world, in the main known to ourselves alone, and in either of these we may find illustrations and examples of this sin of selfishness only too many. What selfishness in high places and in low —among the rich, and among the poor! I have seen it asserted of our artisans, that, earning such large wages as they do, on an average one-third of their weekly earnings is spent on selfish gratifications in which it is impossible that their wives and children can share. Nor have those in higher places a right to cast a stone at these, while so much of their superfluity, of that which God lent them, but did not give, ministers to their own luxury, their own pride of life, so little of it to the urgent needs of Christ's suffering poor; while of their energies, their time, their thoughts, so much is devoted to their own interests and amusements, so little, if indeed any part at all, to bettering the condition, or alleviating the sorrows of others.

We all, my brethren, hate selfishness in the abstract; we count it an ugly sin, when we see it plainly stamped on the lives and actions of others. The Oriental despot, who appropriates a hundred wives to himself, and thus compels a hundred of his subjects to have no wife at all, seeing that there are not more women born into the world than men; the slaveowner, who robs his fellow-men of their dearest rights, and compels them to a lifelong servitude and toil, not for their own profit but for his; the seducer of innocence who, for a moment's vile gratification, poisons the springs of a life, turns all its sweet into bitter, its glory into shame; these and such as these are hateful spectacles, and more or less we all feel them to be such. But it would be ill done, if in our abhorrence of more glaring and ugly selfishnesses such as these, to some of which we are not tempted, others of which are quite out of our reach, we lost sight of the thousand subtler, and therefore more dangerous, forms in which this same sin seeks to penetrate and insinuate itself into the life of every one among us. For, indeed, such thousand subtler, more insinuating forms it has; and much, very much in the arrangements of society, in the recognized maxims of the world, in the corruptions of our own hearts, is ever disposing us to give it allowance and acceptance, when it suggests, as it is ever doing, that we should take the ease, and give another the toil; we should take the safety, and give another the danger; we should take the honour, and give another the dishonour; we should take the pleasure, and give another the pain; we should take the profit, and give another the loss.

But if it be indeed true, as the Apostle so mournfully asserts—namely, that, except in so far as they are under the leading of the Spirit, 'all men seek their own;'

if selfishness be this familiar evil, this domestic foe, lurking so close to every one of us, ever endeavouring to lead us away from the path of self-denial and self-sacrifice to that of self-seeking and self-pleasing, how shall we resist it, how shall we overcome it? St. Paul gives us a clear hint how this may be done, when having said, 'Look not every man on his own things, but every man also on the things of others,' he goes on to say, 'Let this mind be in you, which was also in Christ Jesus;' and then sets before us, in those wonderful words which follow my text, the great pattern and example of his life and of his death. He was rich, yet for our sakes He made Himself poor; He was in the form of God, yet He took on Him the form of a servant. All might, majesty, glory, and dominion were his; He was in the bosom of the Father; He shared with the Father and the Holy Ghost in the incommunicable bliss of Deity; yet all this He laid aside; all this He renounced, and became a man—that had been much, that had been an infinite condescension; but more than this—of men the least and the last, a worm and no man; for three and thirty years He trod this painful earth of ours, despised, rejected, an outcast of his people, crowning at length that painful life with a death as full of indignity as of anguish. And for what? for whom? For nothing that should accrue to Himself, but for us men and for our salvation, that we by his poverty might be rich, by his stripes might be healed, that his shame might be our glory, his cross our crown, his death our life. I say, brethren, that the contemplation of Christ, not a cold, formal reception of certain doctrines, but a contemplation of Him, an habitual realizing of Him to our spiritual eye, first in the glory which He had with the Father before the foundation of the world, all which He laid down for our sakes; and then in his earthly life of poverty, of labour, of humiliation, of scorn, of suffering, of death, all which He undertook for our sakes; it is this, brought home to us by that Spirit who can take of the things of Christ and show them unto us, which must cure us (for nothing else will) of our selfish preference of ourselves to others, of that seeking of our own things and not the things also of others, which now clings and cleaves, like an inner garment, so closely to us all.

And if, dear friends, we are resolved to walk in that more excellent way in which we have Him for our pattern and our guide, do not let us wait for great and signal opportunities of shewing that we can prefer the good of others to our own. Such occur very seldom; while small occasions occur every day, in the bosom of our family, in our daily intercourse with the world; and moreover, strange as this may sound, the great occasions are not nearly so good a test of our sincerity as the small. Great acts of self-sacrifice attract observation, are talked about, often bring honour, credit, glory to the doer. A thousand mixed motives may impel us to these; but the smaller acts in which we yield our will to the will of others, postpone our convenience, our pleasure, our ease, to theirs, these, unobserved by the world, often unobserved even by the person on whose behalf they are done, these are a far truer test. Let us then, every one, ask ourselves at once such questions as these, Am I shifting off upon some other a burden which I ought to bear? Do I habitually inflict large inconvenience and toil upon others for the sake of some trifling convenience or pleasure which may accrue to myself? What is the distribution of my time, what of my money? Is it a selfish one? Is self the centre, round which I seek to make that little world in which I move, so far as in me lies, to revolve? Do I live in habitual disregard of the Apostle's precept, 'Look not every man on his own things, but also on the things of others'? And oh! remember the danger which lies so near us in such a self-examination as this, lest while we are sharpsighted as eagles to see the motes in the eyes of our brethren, we should be blind as moles to see the beams in our own. Unless our eyes are anointed with eyesalve, with the eyesalve to be bought of Christ, we shall see nothing here. The selfishness, most visible to all the rest of the world, will escape ourselves, unless

He shews it to us. But He will shew it, if we honestly seek this at his hands; and not this only, but will go on to teach us the blessed art of so losing our lives in this world, that we may save them unto life eternal.

SERMON XI.

ON THE DUTY OF HATING VAIN THOUGHTS.

Psalm cxix. 113.
I hate vain thoughts.

How many are there among us who could confidently take up the Psalmist's words, and make them our own; and in his sight, and speaking as in the immediate presence of Him to whom all hearts, and all the imaginations of all hearts, are open and manifest, could say, 'I hate vain thoughts'? I fear not all; perhaps very few indeed. For indeed how many, while they acknowledge a certain rule on their outward conduct, and that their actions must be conformed to a law imposed on them from above, seem to take for granted that thoughts are free, that these may move in that inner region and province which is peculiarly their own, unquestioned and unchallenged; that they will have to give little or no account of these.

And yet Scripture does not encourage us in any such notion as this. The wickedness of the old world, that wickedness which only a Flood could wash away, how is that set forth to us there? Not so much by the evil which was done, as by the evil which was thought. 'God saw,' we are told, 'that every imagination of the thoughts of man's heart was only evil continually.'[1] What does St. Peter say to Simon Magus? 'Pray God, if perhaps the thought of thine heart may be forgiven thee.'[2] And does not another Apostle remind us that the Word of God is 'a discerner of the thoughts and intents of the heart';[3] that the Lord at his coming 'both will bring to light the hidden things of darkness, and will make manifest the counsels of the hearts: and then shall every man have praise of God'?[4]

But what need I to accumulate proofs that, as God is a knower of the thoughts of men's hearts, so also is He a punisher of those which are evil? Often, it is true, thoughts present themselves to us as such slight, shadowy, evanescent things, coming and going, and, as we fancy, leaving no trace behind them, that we fail altogether to attach to them the importance which they deserve. And yet, dear brethren, what is a word or deed but an embodied thought? the incarnation, if I may so speak, of a thought? And must not the thought of a man, as the primary and immediate birth of his heart, be more truly indicative, tell more clearly what is in him, than his words or works, which are only

---

[1] Gen. vi. 5.   [2] Acts viii. 22.
[3] Heb. iv. 12.   [4] 1 Cor. iv. 5.

secondary outcomings of the man, can ever do? Reason, then, there is enough that we should set a watch not merely at the door of our lips, and over the works of our hands, but that we keep a watch closer still, one which will demand a yet stricter vigilance; ever striving and ever praying that the meditation of our hearts may be acceptable in God's sight; and, as a needful condition of this, hating 'vain thoughts,' which cannot be acceptable to Him.

But what, it may be asked, is included in this phrase, 'vain thoughts'? This question, I propose to answer first; and then, this answered, to consider, very briefly, what are some of the helps which we may use, and where we may find such helps, for the fighting against, overcoming, and in the end getting rid of these.

And first, what are 'vain thoughts'? To this it may be answered in the general, that as there are three forms of temptation by which we are assailed in other regions of our spiritual life, as there is no sin which does not range itself under one or other of these three heads, which is not a yielding to the world, or to the flesh, or to the devil, so fares it also in that region with which we have now particularly to do, the region of the thoughts.

And, first, there are the vain *worldly* thoughts,

which we must hate. And here, let me observe by the way, that thoughts, which in themselves are perfectly harmless and innocent, may become vain through being welcomed and entertained at the wrong season. Thoughts, for example, of the shop, of the market, of the exchange—no one would affirm that these in themselves are vain; they belong to the necessary business of many men; allowable, and more than allowable, in their place and in their time; but yet they may become 'vain,' if suffered to intrude, without rebuke, on our prayers, to follow us to the house of God, it may be to the very table of the Lord, and in other ways to disturb the holy seventh-day rest of our spirits; if we do not resolutely shut the door of the inner chamber of our hearts against them when we would pray to our Father in heaven.

So, too, these same thoughts may become sinful and vain through mere excess, through occupying our minds overmuch; as when we dwell on them exclusively; at our uprising and downsitting; when they are with us at all times of the day; when we do not care to dismiss them, and indeed could hardly now dismiss them if we tried. The world must be very near us, when the worldly thought is ever with us. Our treasure, our best treasure, must assuredly be there, else our heart and the thought of our heart would not be always there also. I suppose that every one who wishes to deepen and strengthen his own spiritual life, proposes to himself some sort of meditation on things heavenly at some set time of every day; but what chance has this meditation of holding its place, what likelihood is there that it will not presently be wholly thrust out of the day, when worldly thoughts, grown strong by too much allowance, are ever ready to dispute with it even that brief interval which it would fain claim for itself? Or even if they should not wholly expel it, they will leave it a dead heartless thing, with all power, grace, and strength departed from it. See then, I would beseech you, that that which in itself may be perfectly right do not, through excess and overmuch allowance, become wrong to you. You are in the world, and have your work to do in the world; and that work should be done vigorously and well, and this it cannot be without due thought bestowed upon it; moreover, as interesting and concerning you nearly, it *must* often recur to your mind. Yet for all this have a care that it do not swallow you up, that it do not take possession of you altogether. Thoughts that are *always* running on this world, on its hopes and fears, its gains and losses, its victories and defeats, that can never get out of this track, are vain thoughts; and he that is wise will see betimes the peril and the danger with which they threaten the whole life of his soul, and will watch against them, as knowing that we may perish through things lawful as surely as through things unlawful.

But if a wise man will watch against these thoughts about this world, which are only sinful when indulged and allowed at a wrong time or in excess, how much more will he hate those that in their nature and essence are sinful; as, for example, *impure* thoughts; being such as more than any other sully and defile the mirror of the soul, and render it incapable of giving back the pure image of God. What a call there is not to eschew only but to hate such on the part of those who profess to be followers of the immaculate Lamb, of the Prince of all purities, of Him who has said, 'Be ye holy, for I am holy;' and who, when He demands holiness on the part of his people, does not contemplate a mere blamelessness in outward conversation, so that men shall see nothing amiss in them, but that holiness of heart which shall endure his searching glance, before whom all things are naked and manifest. Hate, then, these 'vain thoughts'; hate them with a perfect hatred. They are in themselves a whole world of iniquity, and do more perhaps than evil thoughts of any other kind to taint, corrupt, and poison the whole inner life of the soul, until nothing there is pure, but everything defiled.

The transition to other thoughts, to such as we more immediately ascribe to the devil, is easy. The connexion between those at which I have just been glancing and these is closer than we might at first imagine. Shakespeare knew this when he made Iago, being as he is the most devilish character which has issued from the wondrous workshop of his brain, also in imagination the uncleanest. Neither is it only in the land of the Gadarenes that devils and swine are found in closest relation with one another. But into this mysterious connexion I will not seek to enter further.[1] It will be enough to indicate *proud* thoughts in general, as the third division of those which I have undertaken to consider. It is only little which I can speak of these.

Few persons in this world obtain as much homage, respect, observance from others as they fain would obtain; few occupy places in this world as high as it seems to themselves their merits and services might justly challenge and deserve. But of these, thus disappointed and defeated of their proper rights, how many make it up to themselves, or at least seek some compensation, in imagining to themselves the course of this world as they would like it to be, or as they hope it may yet one day prove; and the Tempter in fantastic vision is ever at hand to feed these high thoughts of ours, to set us on the high mountain of our pride, to bring half the world to our feet, as ready to do homage to us; for he well knows that there is nothing which more unfits us for

[1] Matt. viii. 30, 31.

humble every-day duties, for prayer, for communion with God, than the indulgence in these vain conceits, and walking in imagination on these high places of our pride. Young men, young women, beware of allowing yourselves in idle daydreams such as these. There may seem to you no harm in them; but there is great and serious harm. Examine them a little closer. Are they not always for the exaltation of self? Is not self the centre of them in every case? It is *you*, not anybody else, but always *you*, who in that imaginary scene which you depict to yourself, are the central figure; you, who do something clever, or grand, or heroic, or self-denying, and obtain the applause and admiration of the world. Can anything be worse, can anything be more injurious to the spiritual life of the soul, to its simplicity and purity, than these secret glorifyings of self? Can anything do greater wrong to the soul than this substitution of magnificent feats of imaginary heroism or self-denial for the commonplace, every-day tasks and humbler duties of the Christian life, which are really within our power, and which claim fulfilment at our hands? Hate, then, these vain thoughts. They will fill you with conceit of the worst kind, and leave you empty of every good thing.

But, still more evidently devilish, there are 'vain thoughts' of malice and evil-will; these too growing out of a root of pride, as it would not be difficult to show. It is strange that persons should ever wish ill to others gratuitously, and without having received any slight or wrong at their hands. Yet so it is, nothing perhaps revealing so strongly the depth of man's fall, and the way in which the poison of the Old Serpent has penetrated into the veins, as the fact that there is such a thing as 'being glad at calamities' (the Greek language has a word for this gladness), and this even though the calamity of others bring no profit to us, and though they whom the calamity has overtaken have never in anything harmed or wronged us in the least. There is such a thing as looking abroad on the world, and grudging to see others more prosperous, more esteemed, happier in their family circle, in higher estate, more at ease in their outward circumstances; and desiring that this prosperity should be less, and having pleasure in any event which should make it less, which should justify words like those of the Prophet, 'Art thou also become weak as we? art thou become like unto us?'[1] Hate, I beseech you, these vain thoughts. Let none say in his heart, 'Oh, I could never be tempted to such gratuitous malignity as this.' What any other has ever been tempted to, be sure that you may be tempted to the same; and perhaps, if you had watched yourself a little closer, you would be ready to acknowledge that you had been tempted to it already; and not this only, but had yielded to the temptation.

[1] Isa. xiv. 10.

But a few words must still be spoken on the remedies for 'vain thoughts'; how to resist them, how so effectually to hate them that they shall find no room nor entertainment with us. It is plain that before we undertake this in earnest, we must be fully aware of their guilt. I have attempted to say something of this already, and cannot now say more. Let it be sufficient once again to remind you, that in that day which may be so near, which cannot be very remote, God shall judge not the open things only of men's lives, but the secrets of men's hearts, by Jesus Christ.

Then, too, let us fully realize to ourselves the ever-present danger which there is, that the evil thought will breed something even worse than itself. 'Lust, when it hath conceived, bringeth forth sin.' The evil thought is mother of the evil deed. It is the cockatrice's egg, from which the fiery flying serpent may at any moment be born. No man can say, with confidence, 'Thus far will I advance in sin, but no farther. I will taste, in imagination, the sweetness of the sin; but there I will stop.' God evermore defeats these wicked calculations of ours; and the sin which we have deliberately resolved to commit in part, He compels us (for I will not shrink from using the word) to commit in the whole.

But this the guilt and the danger of allowing such thoughts as these freely admitted, how shall we rid ourselves of them? how shall we chase them away? Chase them *wholly* away, we never shall; but, as an old divine said well, 'I cannot hinder a bird from flying over my head, but I can hinder it from building its nest in my hair.' Let them find no entertainment from us. As often as they visit us, let them drive us to Him, by whose holy inspiration alone we are able either to think those things which be good, or to refuse to think those things which be evil; let them, I say, drive us to Him in a real, though it may be a voiceless prayer, in a brief meditation on the glories of heaven, or on the pains of hell, or on Christ hanging upon his cross and bearing there the penalty of our sins, or on Christ coming to judgment and bringing to light all hidden things of darkness and this wicked thought of ours among the rest. In devices such as these we must find our help. Nor may we doubt that the issue and reward of all manful resistance to him from whom all evil things do come, and these fiery flying darts among the rest, will be that he will flee from us; and that to us too it will be granted to enter into and a little to understand the blessedness of those words which had their first and most glorious fulfilment in the wilderness and for the Lord, 'Then the devil leaveth him, and, behold, angels came and ministered unto him.'[1]

[1] Matt. iv. 11.

SERMON XII.

PONTIUS PILATE.

MATT. xxvii. 11.
And Jesus stood before the governor.

Of the many evil men who were immediate sharers in the guilt of our Lord's death, there is none who affords such a study of character as Pontius Pilate; none, the inner workings of whose heart and mind we are allowed so closely to inspect. As this study of character he is the more profitable to us, because, among many guilty, he is by no means the guiltiest; his sin, which we may sum up in the words, 'moral cowardice,' much more closely resembling the sin into which any one of us at any moment *may* fall, into which every one of us has fallen, than the sin of Judas Iscariot or of Caiaphas.

The three earlier Evangelists deal in a rapid and summary manner with this portion of the Evangelical story. It is for this reason that St. John treats it at full. Profoundly interesting is it to note, as traced by him, the mortal duel which is fought out between the Roman Governor and the Jewish hierarchs; a duel which is not the less real, nor waged the less fiercely, because carried on under forms which partially veil it from our eyes, so that only at certain moments the intense hostility which animates both him and them is permitted to appear. This conflict is undecided long, but the Jewish hierarchs are victorious in the end. And no wonder. They know their own minds, while he only half knows his. They are consistent, thorough-going in evil; he is weak and less than half-hearted in good. No sooner do they stand face to face than the mutual antipathy breaks forth, and the struggle at once begins. They have brought their prisoner to him, with the demand which, if not openly made, it is impossible for Pilate to miss, that without more ado he should confirm the sentence which they have already passed upon Him. But Pilate is not wholly without that sense of law and of the dignity of law which had given to the Romans the dominion of the world; which speaks out so proudly in the words of another Roman Governor, 'It is not the manner of the Romans to deliver any man to die, before that he which is accused have licence to answer for himself concerning the crime laid against him;'[1] and therefore going out to them he demands, 'What accusation bring ye against this man?' This question, revealing as it does his resolution not to be made a blind instrument of their malice, offends them greatly. They would fain

[1] Acts xxv. 16.

enter into no discussion. What they want is that the Governor, accepting the justice of their sentence, should proceed to execute it, or give them authority to do so. They reply in displeasure, 'If he were not a malefactor, we would not have delivered him up unto thee.' It was enough that they of the Great Sanhedrim had condemned Him; let the Roman Governor ratify their sentence and carry it out; that is his business. 'If this be so; if He be indeed a malefactor, as you say,' Pilate replies, 'carry out yourselves the sentence which ye have pronounced against Him. Take Him, and judge Him after your law.' There would have been nothing more welcome to them than this permission, but for one fact, which he knew and which they knew; and which no doubt was present in his mind when he so spake—namely, that the right of capital punishment, the power of the sword, had been withdrawn from them by the Romans, and it was the life of the Lord they desired. And now they are brought to the humiliating confession of this; a confession which must have cost them much, and to which, for this very reason, Pilate is the better pleased to bring them, 'It is not lawful for us to put any man to death.' Neither can they any longer hope that he will be content to be the mere passive executor of their will; they proceed therefore at once to bring forth their charges against the Lord.

To St. Luke we owe an exact account of the shape

which these charges took: 'We found this fellow perverting the nation, and forbidding to give tribute to Cæsar, saying that he himself is Christ a King.'[1] They knew very well, cunning and malignant as they were, that they would very hardly indeed persuade Pilate to put Jesus to death on the ground that He had claimed to be the Son of God; that his first impulse would be to drive them, bringing this accusation, from his judgment-seat with something of the same contempt with which Gallio drove the accusers of St. Paul.[2] They can scarcely hope to effect their end without giving a political colouring to his offence. It must not be one so much against their theocracy as against the civil government of Rome. And this colouring with infinite dexterity they give to their charge. Christ did claim to be a King; and they took for granted that, if He should be questioned whether He were such or not, He would not deny it. Their hope was (nor were they altogether disappointed in this hope), that Pilate, with the quick ear of suspicion, would catch at that word 'king,' and, not perceiving how profoundly different his kingdom was from any of the kingdoms of the world, and in how different a sense He claimed to be a King, would at once see in Jesus a competitor for the throne of Judæa, a troublesome and, it might be, a dangerous pretender, whom it would be well with the least delay

[1] xxiii. 2.   [2] Acts xviii. 15.

or noise to get out of the way. There is an infinite baseness in the manner in which they thus offer up their own expectations of a Messiah, prostituting these to their more urgent purpose of hate and revenge, in their charging against the Lord the very thing which they were waiting and hoping that the Messiah, such as they expected Him, would do—namely, that He would rally the whole nation against the hated domination of the Gentile. The same cunning malignity, the same making of the charge a political one, reappears more than once in the Acts.[1]

They have succeeded so far that, as all the four Evangelists tell us, Pilate begins his judicial inquiry with the question, 'Art thou the King of the Jews?' But while the three earlier Evangelists report only the Lord's simple affirmation that such He was, St. John records a most important conversation between Him and Pilate. The Governor, having again withdrawn into the judgment-hall, whither the Jews did not follow, and having called the Lord unto him, addressed this question about his kingship to Him. Instead of answering at once, He replies to question with question: 'Sayest thou this thing of thyself, or did others tell it thee of me?' as much as to say, 'In what spirit dost thou ask this question? for when I know this, I shall better know what reply I shall make to it. Is it the

[1] See xvi. 21; xvii. 6, 7.

true Messiah-hope which thou art asking after? or art thou merely retailing the accusations made against Me by my enemies?' Not, alas! 'of himself.' The proud Roman indignantly puts back the suggestion that he could take any interest in the Jewish hope of a Messiah and Saviour. 'Am I a Jew,' is his displeased rejoinder to the supposition that he should have spoken this of himself, 'that I should care for such dreams and expectations as these which thy people cherish? Thine own nation and the Chief Priests have delivered Thee unto me; and therefore I have put this question to Thee.' And then, as one offended at the freedom of that question, he resumes the judge; but at the same time with something of good-will he asks, 'What hast thou done?' The Lord shall thus have his opportunity of explaining the bitter enmity which the chiefs of his own nation thus manifested against Him. He must have done something to provoke this enmity. What was it?

The answer of the Lord is not direct, but indirectly He does reply. 'You ask Me what I have done? Nothing punishable by the laws of any state; nothing of which the state can take cognizance, seeing that my kingdom, for I am a King, is not a kingdom of this world; is not from hence, grows out of no earthly root.' He does not, as all who are capable of judging will at once acknowledge, deny that his kingdom is *here*, but only that it is *hence*, that it is from beneath; being, as it indeed is, from above; a kingdom coming down from heaven, however the seat of it may be for a while upon earth; in the words of Augustine, 'Non negat *hic* esse, sed *hinc*.' Observe, I beseech you by the way, the majestic confidence with which, even at that hour, when abandoned by all, in the hands of foes, He who, in the words of St. Paul, 'witnessed a good confession before Pontius Pilate,' not once only, but thrice, claims a kingdom as properly his own.

His words, 'If my kingdom were of this world, then would my servants fight, that I should not be delivered to the Jews,' have been often misunderstood. They are often taken to explain the passive tameness with which the disciples allowed their Lord to be laid hold of in the garden of Gethsemane, not offering more than the faintest shadow of resistance; indeed, for the greater part, offering none. But the words cannot bear this meaning. They refer not to the past, but to the present. 'Were my kingdom of this world, then would my servants now interfere, that thou shouldst not give Me back to the power of the Jews.' And by these 'servants' He means, not that feeble, terrified little band of Apostles, with their 'two swords,'[1] nor yet the unwarlike train of his followers; but He has in his mind's eye those 'twelve legions' of angels of whom He spake a

[1] Luke xxii. 38.

little while before, whom and more than whom his Father at a word of his would give Him.[1] He saw, though Pilate could not see, the mountain full of horses and chariots of fire, compassing round about the greater than Elisha who was here,[2] which all He might even now at a beck summon to his aid.

You will have observed that Christ has not yet in as many words called Himself a King; but in that three times repeated mention of his kingdom his kingship was virtually implied. Pilate recognizes this, and repeats his question, 'Art thou a king then?' He repeats it; but, if I do not mistake, in another spirit from that in which he put it at the first. The question as now put is rather an evidence of the deep though momentary impression which Christ's last words have made upon the questioner. It is not a judicial interrogation; not a going back on the accusation of the Jews; not as much as to say, 'Then Thou allowest the truth of this charge which they make against Thee.' The inquiry springs from a deeper root, as evidenced by the Lord's reply, 'Thou sayest; for I am a King. To this end was I born'—this had reference to his birth of a woman; 'and for this cause came I into the world'—descended from his Father's throne, laid aside for a while the glory which He had with Him from the beginning, 'that I should bear witness unto the

---

[1] Matt. xxvi. 53.   [2] 2 Kings vi. 17.

truth. Every one that is of the truth heareth my voice.'

Note, I beseech you here, how graciously the Lord, speaking to a heathen, so modifies his language as to be intelligible to him. He speaks of 'the truth,' that being a middle term between Jewish theology and heathen philosophy, common to both, and forming a connecting link between them. He does not speak of the Messias hope, which would have been a wholly unintelligible language to Pilate, but of 'the truth.' All the better and nobler heathen professed themselves lovers and seekers of the truth. If there had been any longing after it in Pilate, that word would have found an echo in his heart. If he had been in any sense 'of the truth,' with any predisposition for it, he would, as Christ says, have heard *his* voice, even his who was Himself the Incarnate Truth. But he has none; and having now rid himself of those momentary impressions, and desiring to break off the discourse, he exclaims with something of impatience and contempt, and as a sceptical child of this present world, 'What is truth?' and then, without waiting for an answer, he returned to the Jewish crowd who were impatiently waiting without, and declared the conviction at which he had arrived, 'I find in him no fault at all.' They renew their charges more fiercely than ever, for they are afraid that their victim will escape them: 'He stirreth up the people, teaching throughout all Jewry, beginning from Galilee to this place.' Pilate eagerly catches at the word Galilee; he would fain disengage himself from the whole affair, in which, as he now plainly sees, he must either act directly against his conscience, condemning an innocent man, or else embitter still more against himself all the chiefs of the Jewish nation. That mention of Galilee seems to open to him an unlooked-for way of escape. Is the man a Galilæan? He will send Him to be judged by Herod, the tetrarch of Galilee, 'who himself also was at Jerusalem at that time.' Here will be a double gain, a compliment paid to Herod, in this acknowledgment of his jurisdiction, in this unwillingness to encroach upon it; and, still better than this, he will so deliver himself from that terrible dilemma in which he is placed. Unhappy man! with what dismay he must presently have seen the prisoner, whom he had hoped to be rid of for ever, returned upon his hands. He was not so to escape.

Weak and without all moral supports, Pilate cannot bring himself, at all costs, to do justice. But there is one way remaining still, by which it may be possible to avoid committing the flagrant injustice which the Jews require at his hands. They had a custom that the Governor should release to them a prisoner at the Passover. He would himself propose that Jesus should be the prisoner. The release of one so remarkable as

He was, one accused of the highest crime against the state, would prove a most solemn recognition on his part of their right to such a privilege—would probably be eagerly grasped at by the people. He knew too that there were many sympathies among the multitude in favour of the Lord, as his triumphal entry into Jerusalem some few days before had sufficiently attested. But there was a competitor for the popular favour, with far stronger claims on that favour than were his; one who had actually done what they had only hoped that Jesus would do—namely, made insurrection against the Roman power, and shed the blood of Roman oppressors; and him the populace are easily moved to ask, instead of the Holy and the Just.

This feeble effort of Pilate to save the Lord, or rather to save himself from that miserable guilt which he sees so close before him, has failed. He has still one device behind: he will chastise, and having chastised, will release Him. Assuredly some movements of compassion will stir in their hearts when they behold Him torn and bleeding under the cruel Roman rods; or if not movements of compassion, yet of contempt, which shall do the work of pity; and he hopes to take advantage of these, so to effect his release. Such is his scheme for befriending the Lord. Truly, the tender mercies of the wicked are cruel. Pilate withdraws; and now begins the scene of insult and wrong and cruel mocking which has imprinted itself so deeply on the heart and imagination of Christendom, but to dwell on which would be foreign to the purpose of to-day. All this was transacted within the prætorium, or inner court of Pilate's house, out of sight therefore of the Jewish multitude, who were eagerly waiting without.

And now Pilate, in pursuance of his scheme, will make his final effort to stir some feeling of commiseration in their hearts. Is it not enough? he would imply; the man is innocent; the inquisition by scourging has wrung out from him no confession of guilt, of any plots against the Roman sovereignty, or against his own countrymen. And 'then came Jesus forth' in his forlorn masquerade of royalty, 'wearing the crown of thorns and the purple robe.' Pilate himself leads Him forth, and shows Him to the people, uttering at the same time that wondrous word which the Church has so eagerly caught up; for just as Caiaphas, the representative of the Jewish Church, spake deeper things than he knew when he exclaimed, 'It is expedient for us that one man should die for the people,'[1] even so Pilate, the representative of the heathen world, spake a far deeper word than he was aware of, when, pointing to the Prince of Martyrs, he exclaimed, *'Ecce homo!'*—'Behold the man!' What Pilate himself

[1] John xi. 50.

meant, what emphasis *he* laid on the words, it is not easy to determine; yet no doubt for the moment he was touched and moved, however there may have mingled contempt with the pity. We may supplement, I think, his 'Behold the man' with some such words as these,—' whom you dread so much; whom you would fain have me to dread so much.'

But the rude Roman, nursed among conflicts and blood, familiar with the horrid butcheries of the Roman amphitheatre, seeks in vain to touch the hearts of Jewish Priests. Their only answer is, 'Crucify him, crucify him!' Pilate replies, 'Take ye him, and crucify him: for I find no fault in him.' With a bitter irony the Governor again affects to forget that this power had passed from them. They are humiliating him, and he in return will humiliate them, obliging them to confess that they must wait upon a heathen tribunal for the carrying out of their decrees, even those which most nearly concern the highest matters of their faith. And he does bring them to this. He has so plainly declared that on political grounds he can find no guilt in their prisoner, that the Roman State was in nothing aggrieved or threatened by Him, as to leave them no alternative; they must drop this accusation altogether, and come back from this, the pretended charge, to the real one; and this now they do: 'He may have done nothing against your law, but He has against ours. By our law He ought to die, because He made Himself the Son of God.'

How significant are the words which follow. 'When Pilate therefore heard that saying, he was *the more afraid*.' So that there had already woke up in him some mysterious awe, awe which had deepened into fear, in respect of this prisoner before him; but now he was 'the more afraid.' That word, 'Son of God,' alarmed him. All the unbelief of the time, all the scepticism of his own heart, had not so entirely destroyed in him every vestige of faith in a higher world, and one in closest connexion with this lower, but that this sounded as a word of fear in his ears. What if he should be drawing down some special vengeance of heaven upon himself, outraging One who had both the power and the will to avenge himself? And then there may have come again to his mind the message of his wife, not so much heeded at the moment, 'Have thou nothing to do with that just man: for I have suffered many things this day in a dream because of him.'[1] Again he pauses; withdraws once more with the Lord into the judgment-hall, and with direct reference to those words, 'Son of God,' demands of Him, 'Whence art thou?' 'Dost Thou,' that is, 'claim to belong to another and higher world than this?' To this question Jesus gives him no answer. He knows too surely what the end will be,

[1] Matt. xxvii. 19.

and will not increase Pilate's guilt by increasing his knowledge. The Roman Governor is offended at this silence. 'Speakest thou not unto me? knowest thou not that I have power to crucify thee, and have power to release thee?' In one sense this was true, but in another most false. A righteous judge has no power— I mean morally he has none—to condemn the innocent, or to absolve the guilty. He is set to execute judgment and righteousness upon earth. And our Lord, in his reply, would fain bring Pilate back to this, the rightful view of his office: 'Thou couldest have no power at all against me, except it were given thee from above; therefore he that delivered me unto thee hath the greater sin.' Difficult words, but which I think may thus be explained: 'Thou speakest as though I were delivered into thy hands, for thee to do with Me as thou wilt. But it is not so. Thou hast just that amount of power which is granted thee from above; that much, and no more. Thou knowest not, or only dimly and obscurely knowest this, as compared with him, the Jewish High Priest,'—representative here of the whole body of Christ's Jewish enemies,—'who, with clearer light and ampler knowledge, have risen up against Me, and delivered Me into thine hands; whose sin, therefore, is greater than thine.' Wonderful indeed is the manner in which the Lord at such a moment measures out the comparative guilt of one and another, of Jewish High

Priest and Roman Governor; and graciously places in the mildest possible light his guilt, who was just about to send him to a cruel and unrighteous death.

This word of Christ has found out Pilate in such inmost depths of his heart, that 'from thenceforth he sought to release him;' but as he had done this already, we can only understand that now he did it more earnestly than ever; in St. Peter's words ' he was determined to let him go.'[1] And perhaps he might have ventured something in the cause of righteousness and truth; but an accusation at Rome, and to Tiberius, the most suspicious of all tyrants, this he could not brave; and it is with this that the Jewish chief priests threaten him now. They have kept this weapon in their armoury to the last, only to bring it forth in case of uttermost need, and when every other has failed. But this need has arrived, and they do not scruple to employ it: 'If thou let this man go, thou art not Cæsar's friend: whosoever maketh himself a king speaketh against Cæsar.' They will charge him at Rome with this his unseasonable lenity to a rebel and a pretender to Cæsar's throne. So much they make Pilate clearly to understand, and this is enough. They have thrown a weight into the scale of unrighteousness and wrong, which causes that of righteousness and truth at once to kick the beam. His guilty conscience tells him that, even if in this

[1] Acts iii. 13.

matter he could clear himself, there were charges enough of malversation, of violence, of cruelty, which they could bring against him, and from which it would be impossible to clear himself. He was prepared to drive matters far, but he dared not drive them so far as this. 'When Pilate therefore heard that saying, he brought Jesus forth,' and with one more bitter word to the Jewish priests, 'Shall I crucify your king?' which drew from them one shameful disavowal more of all their hopes of a Messiah, 'We have no king but Cæsar,' he delivered Jesus unto them to be crucified. At the same time he takes care to embody his mockery, not of the Lord, but of the persecutors of the Lord, in the title which he wrote and fixed upon the cross, 'Jesus of Nazareth the King of the Jews;' being only the better pleased, and the more determined not to alter it, when he found that, as he had intended, they took it as an insult to themselves.[1]

And so ends the tragedy of Pontius Pilate,—a bad man, but by no means the worst of that wonderful group which are gathered round the cross of Christ, and on whom that cross has poured such a flood of light; who, as actors, abettors, or approvers, share the primary guilt of that crime, the secondary guilt of which is shared by us all. A bad man, but very far from the worst; with a guilt which reaches not at all to the guilt of

[1] John xix. 21, 22.

high priests ; which stands far below that of Judas ; and therefore the more awful example of the crimes in which men may be entangled merely through a lack of moral stamina ; for who can attest to us with such a dreadful clearness as he does, how little feeble motions towards good will profit, nay, how they will serve only to deepen the damnation of those who refuse to yield obedience to them ; who, seeing what is the better part, do yet for by-ends of worldly policy and convenience, and to make things safe and pleasant to themselves, shrink from the painfulness of duty, and leaving that better part, choose the worse ?

SERMON XIII.

THE DEATH AND BURIAL OF MOSES.

DEUT. iv. 21, 22.

Furthermore the Lord was angry with me for your sakes, and sware that I should not go over Jordan, and that I should not go in unto that good land, which the Lord thy God giveth thee for an inheritance: But I must die in this land, I must not go over Jordan: but ye shall go over, and possess that good land.

WHO is there that does not feel, as he reads or hears these words, the deep pathos of them? There is no faintest murmur, no lightest note of complaint, in the language with which the aged servant of God records his own sentence of exclusion from the Promised Land; yet there pierces an infinite sadness through that language. It is evident that he deeply felt, even while he meekly accepted, the just but severe sentence of his doom. Severe indeed! the entrance into that Promised Land, the bringing in to it of that people for whom he had so long laboured, and wept, and prayed, that should have been the crown of his life, the rich reward of all his toils. Forty years a fugitive and exile in the land of Midian, this long exile the penalty of a too hasty attempt to do in the flesh what he should hereafter accomplish in the spirit;[1] forty years the painful leader of a discontented, murmuring, rebellious people, through a weary and dreadful wilderness; he had borne all their burden, all the contradiction of sinners, all their waywardness, ingratitude, revolt. It was due, under God, to his patience, to his wisdom, to his courage, that one by one the obstacles in his path and theirs had been all cleared away; that the mountains had become plains; and now, when the glorious goal was in sight, nay, close at hand, as within his grasp, he was not to reach it after all. He had sown, and another should reap; he had laboured, and another should enter into his labours. There was surely, brethren, something deeply tragic in such a defeat of such a life, even though that defeat reached but to this present world, and left untouched the inheritance, incorruptible and undefiled, which was reserved in heaven for him to whom the earthly inheritance was denied.

We know that this with which the Lord had threatened him on the day when he offended by the waters of Meribah,[2] that this which Moses speaks of as the sentence impending over him, was all fulfilled. It is all recorded in the closing chapter of this book. And yet, though the sentence stood fast, it had its gracious mitigations, as the Lord is ever gracious to discover such, when it is

---

[1] Exod. ii. 11-15.   [2] Num. xx. 12.

his own whom He is chastening. 'Get thee up,' it is said to him, 'unto Mount Nebo, which is over against Jericho, and behold the land of Canaan, which I give to the children of Israel for a possession.' And then we are told that 'Moses went up from the plains of Moab unto the mountain of Nebo, to the top of Pisgah, and the Lord shewed him all the land of Gilead, and all Naphtali, and the land of Ephraim, and Manasseh, and all the land of Judah, unto the utmost sea, and the south, and the plain of the valley of Jericho, the city of palm trees, unto Zoar.' A glorious spectacle, a magnificent prospect for any eyes, as the very few, travellers and pilgrims, who have had the opportunity of beholding it, with one consent have declared. But what a spectacle for him! He saw the land, not merely in its natural beauty, a land flowing with milk and honey, a land of mountains and brooks, a land which was the glory of all lands; but he saw it as the land which the Lord had given to Abraham, and Isaac, and Jacob, and to their seed, to the end that, despite of all the sin and opposition of men, even of those who were the bearers of his promises, He might there work out the eternal purposes of his love; that He might found there a fortress of true religion, where his worship should be maintained during the long and weary ages in which all the rest of the world should be wholly given to idolatry; and from whence, in due time, should go forth the ambassadors of his grace, who should everywhere declare his name, and plant the banners of the faith in every land.

And as he saw it, and understood, if not all, yet much of the significance of that land for all the after-history of mankind, how it should be indeed a Holy Land, for it should be once trodden by the feet of One, a prophet like unto him, and greater than him, for He should be Moses and Joshua in one, and far more than either, far more than both; as he saw this good land, may we not believe that he was comforted for all, felt that it was glory enough for a sinful man to have been used by God to bring his people thus far, even to the verge and border of this land of inheritance? May we not be sure that with him was not merely a perfect acquiescence in the will of God; so that he accepted that will without murmuring or repining; but that he felt goodness and mercy to have followed him from the first to the last, and that no good thing had been withholden from him? and that so, looking in that supreme hour before and after, looking back to all the way by which the Lord had led him, to those three mysterious forties into which his life had been divided, the forty years at the court of Pharaoh, the forty years in the land of Midian, and now the forty years in the wilderness; and looking forward to a land of inheritance, fairer, richer, brighter even than that which he now saw, but must never tread, the weary, much-enduring man yielded his spirit to his God; God, as the Jewish rabbis assure us, drawing out that spirit with a kiss; they meaning by this to express their sense of the serene composure, the painless peace of his departure.

And, then, one final honour was in store for him still. No human hands bore the dead Lawgiver and Prophet to his grave, or composed him there. '*He*,' that is God, as we are told, ' buried him in a valley in the land of Moab, but no man knoweth of his sepulchre unto this day;' he whom God buried, according to all likelihood not seeing corruption, and his grave unknown, because probably he was raised from it as soon as laid there; only just tasting the penalty of death, and then that penalty removed ; as would all seem indicated and implied by the apparition of Moses, with Elijah, in a glorified body upon the Mount of Transfiguration.[1] The same also seems pointed at in an obscure passage in the Epistle of St. Jude, where mention is made of the Archangel Michael, that is, of Christ the Prince of Angels, on the one side, and of Satan on the other, disputing about the body of Moses;[2] Satan contending that he, as a sinner, should pay to the uttermost all the penalties of sin, death, and the return to dust which goes along with death; the Archangel Michael, the

---

[1] Matt. xvii. 3.   [2] Jude 9.

great Prince which standeth for the children of his people,[1] declaring that for him one part of the penalty, not indeed the essence of it, but this adjunct to it, was remitted.

Let this, however, be as it may, we cannot, I think, read and at all consider this solemn and mysterious close of the great Prophet's life without many thoughts rising in our hearts; without feeling that there are lessons of instruction the most manifold which are presented by it. I shall endeavour very briefly to draw out from it two or three of these.

And first, a life may appear in some leading point of it to have been a failure, to have been defeated of that crowning success which in our shortsighted vision it had almost a right to claim; and may for all this have been a life most acceptable to God, and consummated with a death very precious in his sight. Moses, the saint of the Lord, may lead his people through the wilderness; all the labour, all the toil, may be his; but not, so far as this life is concerned, the recompense and the reward. It is often so. The lives of few men are rounded and complete; there is something wanting, something fragmentary in almost all; and this quite as much in the lives of God's saints as in the lives of other men. They as little realize all in higher things which they propose to themselves, as the children of this world

[1] Dan. xii. 1.

realize all in the meaner objects of ambition which they have proposed to themselves. They carry out precious seed, and sow in tears; but, as regards any harvest in this present time, they often do *not* come again with joy, bringing their sheaves with them. And why? Because God will write his sentence of vanity upon *all* things here. There is *no* labour of men's hands which shall altogether escape this sentence; for sin is an all-pervading element which mingles with *every* work of man's; nothing can altogether escape it; and if it should happen that in these judgments of God any seeming wrong is done to any, if the just expectations of any servant of his may thus seem to have been baffled, He who is the King of ages can redress in eternity the wrongs of time; and all their disappointments and losses here He can there make good for them a thousand fold.

But once more. See in this which the Lord spake unto Moses, 'Thou shalt die in this land; thou shalt not bring this congregation into the land that I have given them,' an example of the strictness with which God will call even his own to account; and, while his judgments are in all the world, will cause them to begin at his own house. Moses' sin seems to us, as we read of it, to have been comparatively a small one, a momentary outbreak of impatience or unbelief, so that he spake unadvisedly with his lips; and yet it entailed this penalty upon him, this baffling of the dearest hopes of his life. Ah, brethren, if these things are done in the green tree, what shall be done in the dry? If judgment thus begin at the house of God, where shall the ungodly and the sinner appear? If God could so punish an act of disobedience, and that so far from a flagrant one, as *we* measure sin, that it has been often disputed wherein exactly the offence of Moses consisted, how shall He deal with those whose whole life is one long disobedience and defiance of Him? Let us take good heed betimes, and separate ourselves not merely from such a doom as theirs, but watch against sins which, falling very far short of their sin, may yet abridge us of our joy, cause us to forfeit some blessed privilege which, except for this, should assuredly have been ours. Moses was dear to God, and this one matter excepted, 'faithful in all his house;' and yet he may not escape; his sin is visited upon him. Surely the service of our God is a very awful thing, much more solemn and awful than we are wont to regard it; not to be done deceitfully; this of course; but neither to be done carelessly, heedlessly, at random. Take we heed to ourselves how we do it. We may not make shipwreck of all, but yet how much we may lose by careless walking, by the allowance of some unmortified corruption. The heavenly inheritance, of God's infinite mercy in Christ, may still be ours, reserved in heaven for us; and yet, while that is saved, how easily may we empty our life of some excellent boon, some crowning and completing good, which it else would have known.

But then, once more. We are wont, and not unnaturally, to regard this death of Moses as something altogether unlike the deaths of other men. And so in a sense it was. The summons to that solitary mountain, every friend and companion left behind, alone with God in that awful solitude, all this is his and no other's. There was indeed something unique in the manner of his departure. And yet, look at it in another point of view, and what was it but the solitude of every death-bed? *On mourra seul,* ' we shall die alone;' these were the words of the great Pascal; and they are true of every man. We may *live* with others, but we must *die* by ourselves. Millions may have gone before us, and millions may follow after; but each one of us must gird himself for that tremendous journey alone; not Moses more lonely on the peak of Nebo; nor of all those weeping ones that stand around our couch, can one, even if he would, take a single step of that journey with us; alone, unless One be with us, a conqueror of Hades, a Prince of Life, who with his rod and staff can comfort those who pass even through the darkest valley of the shadow of death.

Another word, and we will conclude. Observe, I beseech you, and admire the way in which God so often overrules the lives of the saints of the elder covenant, that by them He may, as in type and shadow, set forth to us the eternal verities of the Gospel. So was it here. Moses may lead the people to the borders of the promised land; but he cannot introduce them there, nor give to them that land in possession. Another must do this; and that other, who? Joshua must do this; Joshua or Jesus, for these, as I need not remind you, are forms of the same name. Moses, who gave the law, who received the two tables of stone written with the finger of God, and who declared these to the people, he is the type and embodiment, the visible representative of that law which he gave. 'The law came by Moses;' but yet that law, holy and perfect as it was, could not give life; it could not bring any man into the land of everlasting life, nay, rather, it wrought death. It was 'a fiery law,' terrifying, threatening, scorching, consuming. It could show men what they ought to be; could thus bring them, as it were, to the very borders of the land which they would possess; but it could not of itself make them 'meet for the inheritance of the saints in light.' The law made nothing perfect; but only served as a preface and a prelude for the bringing in of a better hope. Take heed, then, that you hear Moses; that whatever he commands in his moral law you observe and do; yet think not to live thereby, lest it be said to you, as to the Jews of old, 'There is one that accuseth you, even Moses, in whom ye trust.'[1] Thou wilt have come infinitely short of that law which thou hast striven to keep. It will have as infinite condemnation for thee. Think not of Moses that he can ever be more than a schoolmaster to Christ; that he can bring thee a foot further than to the borders of the land of thine inheritance. Another must lead thee in, if ever that good land shall be thine. Jesus, our Joshua, our Saviour, He must do this. He, the Giver of the Spirit; He, the Forgiver of sins, the Deliverer from the curse of the broken law; He, and He only, is the Captain of the Host of the Lord,[2] who can lead through Jordan, who can cast down the walls of Jericho, who can enable his people to take the good land in possession, and to enter upon that everlasting rest which remaineth for the people of God.

[1] John v. 45.   [2] Josh. v. 14.

SERMON XIV.[1]

EVERY GOOD GIFT FROM ABOVE.

JAMES i. 17.

Every good gift and every perfect gift is from above, and cometh down from the Father of lights.

SURELY it has been devised wisely and well that the services of to-day should stand, if possible, in some connexion with the celebrations which will fill up the remainder of the week. You, who have sought that such a connexion should stand plainly forth, have thus declared many things. You have declared first, that you have no intention nor desire to separate the gift from the Giver, to glorify the one, and to forget or leave out of sight the other, to make much of man at the expense of Him who is the God of man, and from whom all the wit, wisdom, intelligence, or goodness that any man has ever possessed, originally came; being, as these are and must be, little fragments, so to speak, of the divine heart or mind. You have declared that for you,

---

[1] Preached at Stratford-upon-Avon, April 24, 1864, being the Tercentenary of Shakespeare's birth.

in the words so opportunely occurring in the service of this morning, ' *every* good gift is from above, and cometh down from the Father of lights;' so truly the Father of *all* Lights, that each other lesser light can only have been derived from his, and must have been kindled first at his authentic fires.

Nor less do you declare that, as all things come of Him, so we are bound to render unto Him thanks for all; and if for the magnificence of that earth which He has framed for man's dwelling-place, for the hills which He has set so fast with his power, for 'this brave overhanging firmament fretted with golden fires,' so it behoves us first and chiefly to praise Him for his most excellent creature man, 'the beauty of the world,' the crown of things, the first-fruits of his creatures; and if for man, then most of all for those men who marvellously transcend their fellows, who, 'framed in the prodigality of nature' or of grace, reveal to us the possibilities of greatness or of goodness which are in man. Yes, apart from all the pleasure or profit which we may have by these, we are bound to praise Him that He has given such gifts unto men, shown them capable of receiving the same; for such is the fellowship of our race, so intimately are we bound up with one another, that what is given to one may in some sort be considered as given to all, and from that one, glory and honour to redound to all.

It has then, doubtless, been well imagined that the sacred services of to-day, in nothing abating their spiritual character, should yet blend themselves, as harmoniously they may, with the other more festal solemnities of the time. One thing only I could willingly have desired, namely, that on some other, less unequal to the occasion, had devolved the task of tracing the connexion between them, and of weaving the one into the other. But it is often our true humility to do what we are bidden, even while we know how imperfectly we shall do it; this rather than to withdraw from the proffered task in that pride which will not endure to attempt anything that it cannot hope to crown with a perfect success. One fitness, indeed, I possess, namely, that I am not wholly unaware of the difficulties of my undertaking. To this I shall address myself now; only first on one or two points challenging your considerate forbearance.

Thus, if I *preach* about Shakespeare, and that method of treatment sounds somewhat novel and unusual in your ears, you will still remember that this is the very thing which I am set to do; which thus in my office as a minister of Christ, and in his holy house, I could alone consent to do. And then if in so doing I pass over innumerable aspects on which he presents himself to us, and contemplate him only upon one; though one, indeed, the most important of all, namely, the directly moral; it is not because other aspects are indifferent to me, or as supposing them indifferent to you; but because here I have no right, as certainly I have no desire, to contemplate him in any other aspect than this.

What reason have we then to celebrate with a jubilee the fact that exactly on this day, three hundred years since, Shakespeare was born? or, to put the question in the form and fashion which this hour and this house will naturally suggest, Why do we thank God, wherein have we just ground to praise Him, that such a man has been among us? What is there in his writings to render them an enduring benefit to us, a possession for ever; such as we feel makes us richer, wiser, and, using it aright, better than we should have been without it? This is the question which I propose a little to consider this morning.

If indeed the literature of a nation were merely an amusement of the cultivated few, the ornament of their idler hours, then what the fashion of it might be, or what manner of men they were who formed it for us, would be of very slight importance indeed; could scarcely at the best afford matter of serious thanksgiving. We might desire that it should be graceful, as we should desire that the garniture of our houses or of our persons should be graceful; that it should entertain without corrupting: our desires could scarcely extend further. But a nation's literature is very much more than this. The work of its noblest and most gifted sons, the utterance of all which has been deepest and nearest to their hearts, it evokes and interprets the unuttered greatness which is latent in others, but which, except for them, would never have come to the birth. By it the mighty heart of a people may be animated and quickened to heroic enterprise and worthiest endeavour. With the breath of strong and purifying emotions, it can stir to a healthy activity the waters of a nation's life, which would else have stagnated and putrefied and corrupted. Having such offices, being capable of such effects as these, of what vast concern it is, that it should deal with the loftiest problems which man's existence presents; solve them, so far as they are capable of solution here; point to a solution beyond the veil, where this only is possible; that, whatever it handles, things high or things low, things eternal or things temporal, spiritual or natural, it should be sound, should be healthy; clear, so far as possible, of offence; enlisting our sympathies on the side of the just and generous, the pure and the true. Of what supreme concern it is that those who so contribute to frame and fashion a nation's life, should be men reconciled with God's scheme of the universe, cheerfully working in their own appointed sphere the work which has been assigned them there, accepting

God's world, because it is his, with all its strange riddles and infinite perplexities, with all the burdens which it lays upon each one of us; not fiercely dashing and shattering themselves, like imprisoned birds, against the bars of their prison-house, or moodily nourishing in their own hearts, and in the hearts of others, thoughts of discontent, revolt, and despair.

Such a poet, I am bold to affirm, we possess in Shakespeare. For must we not, first of all, thankfully acknowledge a healthiness, a moral soundness in all, or nearly all, which he has written? that on his part there is no paltering with the everlasting ordinances on which the moral estate of man's life reposes, no challenging of the fitness of these, no summoning of God to answer for Himself at the bar of man for the world which He has created? Then, too, if he deals with enormous crimes (and he could not do otherwise, for these, alike in fiction and in reality, constitute the tragedy of life); yet the crimes which he deals with travel the common road of human guilt, with no attempt upon his part to extend and enlarge the domain of possible sin, and certainly with no desire to paint it in any other colours than its own. He dallies not with forbidden things. All which the Latin language, with so just a moral instinct, styled *infanda* and *nefanda*, things as little to be spoken of as done, these, which thus declare themselves unutterable, remain with rarest exception unuttered by him.

And in his dialogue, if we set him beside others of his age and time, how little, by comparison with them, is there which we wish away from him, would fain that he had never written. There are some of his contemporaries whose jewels, when they offer any such, must be plucked out of the very mire; who seem to revel in loathsome and disgusting images, in all which, for poor human nature's sake, we would willingly put out of sight altogether. What an immeasurable gulf in this matter divides him from them! while of that which we *must* regret even in him, a part we have a right to ascribe to an age, I will not say of less purity, but of less refinement and coarser than our own; and of that which cannot be thus explained, let us at all events remark how separable almost always it is from the context, leaving, when thus separated, all which remains perfectly wholesome and pure.

There are writers, but Shakespeare is not one of them, whose evil is inwoven with the texture of their writings, with the very web and woof of these; writers who defile everything which they touch; for whom, and ere long for whose readers, nothing is pure, one foul exhalation and miasma of corruption presently enveloping them both. But Shakespeare, if he has wrought any passing wrong, or given any just occasion of offence in the matters of which we speak, let us not forget the compensations which he has made; that we owe to him those ideals of perfect womanhood, which are the loveliest, perhaps the most transcendent, creations of his art. Shakespeare's women, we have but to mention them, and what a procession of female figures, whose very names make music in our ears, move at once before the eyes of our mind. Surely if the woman be in God's intention the appointed guardian of the sanctities of home, the purities of domestic life, we owe him much, who has peopled the world of our imagination with shapes 'so perfect and so peerless' as are these. True it is that we want far more than art, far more than the highest which art can yield, to keep us holy, to preserve us from the sin of our own hearts, from the sin of the world around us; and there is no more fatal mistake than to forget this. Neither dare we affirm of Shakespeare himself that he was always true to those ideals of female loveliness which he had created, that he never broke faith with them. We have evidence, he himself supplies it, evidence, as I think, not to be gainsaid, that there was a period of his life when he laid up much matter of after-sorrow and self-reproach for himself; in his own wonderful words, 'gored his own thoughts, sold cheap what is most dear;' for what so dear as innocency and self-respect? he, too, a diamond only to be polished in its own dust; and, like so many a meaner man, making in one part of his life work too large of repentance for another. But with all this we dare affirm an habitual delight in the purest, the noblest, and the fairest on the part of one who, in the workshop of his imagination, forged a Miranda and an Imogen. 'Filth savours but itself,' feeds, and would fain lead others to feed, on the garbage in which alone it finds pleasure. Of Shakespeare be it said, that he who has painted his long gallery of women, holy, and pure, and good, walking in fearless chastity through the world, has painted, in anything like full length, only one wanton woman, a Cressida, throughout all the ample range of his art, and her only for scorn and contempt.

There is another matter in which, as it seems to me, we owe a large debt of gratitude to Shakespeare, namely, in the fairness, the justice which he displays to all sorts of men, and this even when he was under the strongest temptation to withhold it. He may thus have helped us to something of the same fairness too. Take an example of what I mean. Shakespeare was a true child of the England of the Reformation. He was born of its spirit; he could never have been what he was, if he had not lived and moved in the atmosphere, intellectual and moral, which it had created. Nor was he merely its unconscious product. One who so loved England, 'this demi-paradise,' who dwelt with such affection on the annals of her past glory, who allows the beatings of his own patriot heart to be so clearly felt and seen as he tells the story of Agincourt, could not have been indifferent to the assertion of national independence which the Reformation involved. Indeed, all of us must have felt that we heard not another, but Shakespeare himself, speaking in those grand words with which he makes King John put back the pretensions of a foreign priest to 'tithe and toll' in the dominions of an English king. And yet, born as he was of the spirit of the Reformation, with the after-agitations of that mighty struggle not yet subsided, welcome as would have been to multitudes of his hearers a holding up to hatred or ridicule or contempt of the proud prelate, the scandalous friar, the incontinent nun, there is a noble absence in his writings of everything of the kind. As often as he does introduce members of any religious order, they are full of kindly help for others, and themselves grave, serious, devout. Indeed, we number among these the stately and severe Isabella, who, if she exaggerates aught, does it upon virtue's side. A grand self-respect on the part of the poet will not allow him to fall in with the popular cries, to howl with the wolves, to trample on the weak or the prostrate; and he has helped in this to teach the English people a lesson which they have not altogether failed to learn. That we have here the explanation of what has just been noted, and not in any lingering affection upon his part to Romish doctrines and practices, is clear from the fact that he bears himself exactly in the same fashion towards the Puritans. Here, too, there can be no manner of doubt that any amount of ridicule or abuse of these sectaries, just beginning to make themselves felt and feared, would have been welcome to large numbers of the playgoers of the time, that excellent sport might have been made of all which was peculiar and extravagant in them. Others, indeed, have not scrupled to make it; but, bating a few passing jests with no malice in them, the shafts of his ridicule are never directed against them; nor, indeed, we may take this occasion to add, against any earnest form of religious life whatsoever. He knew too well the danger of confounding the false and the true of religion in a common reproach; and how easily the scorn, meant for the one, might be diverted and made to light upon the other.

But once more: Shakespeare has been found fault with by the critics of the last century, that, as they complain, 'he seems to write without any moral purpose,' that he 'makes no just distribution of good or evil.' It is a shallow view of art, as of life, which could alone have given birth to this accusation. It is true that the moral intention of Shakespeare's poetry does not lie on the surface, is not obtruded; it may and will often escape the careless reader. But it is there, lying deep, as do nearly all the lessons which God teaches us through our own lives, or through the lives of others. To no one of the uninspired writers of the world has it been granted, I believe, so strongly to apprehend, so distinctly to make visible, that men reap as they have sown, that the end lies in the beginning, that sooner or later 'the wheel will come full circle,' and 'the whirligig of time bring round his revenges.' Who else makes us so and with such a solemn awe to feel that justice walks the world—'delaying,' it may be, but 'not forgetting,' as is so often the manner with the divine avengers? Even faults comparatively trivial, like that of Cordelia, he does not fear to shew us what a train of sorrows, for this life at least, they may entail. Certainly we shall look in vain in him, as we look in vain through the moral universe, for that vulgar distribution of rewards and punishments in which some delight; neither is death, but dishonoured life, in his estimate, the worst of ills; for death may be, and often is, an euthanasia, the divine cutting of some tangled knot which no human skill could ever have untied. So, too, if we would recognize these footsteps of God in the world, this Nemesis of life, which he is so careful to trace, we must watch his slightest hints, for in them lies oftentimes the key to, and the explanation of, all. In this, if I may say it with reverence, he often reminds us of Scripture, and will indeed repay almost any amount of patient and accurate study which we may bestow upon him. Let me illustrate what I say. They are but a few idle words dropt at random, which, in the opening scene of *King Lear*, make only too evident that Gloster had never looked back with serious displeasure at the sin of his youth, standing embodied as it does before him in the person of his bastard son; that he still regarded it with complacency, rolled it as a sweet morsel under his tongue. This son, his whole being corroded, poisoned, turned to gall and bitterness, by the ever-present consciousness of the cleaving stain of his birth, is made the instrument to undo him, or rather to bring him through bitterest agonies, through the wreck and ruin of his whole worldly felicity, to a final repentance. Indeed for once Shakespeare himself points the moral in those words, so often quoted, but not oftener than they deserve :—

> 'The gods are just, and of our pleasant vices
> Make instruments to plague us.'

But for this once that he points the moral of a life, a hundred times he leaves us to point it; as indeed is almost always the manner in that Book of books, which, like Joseph's kingly sheaf, stands up in the midst of the field, that so even the chief among the others may do homage to it.

Let me note, in connexion with what has just been spoken, that the ideal characters of his art, just as the real characters of actual life, never stand still. They are rising or falling, growing better or growing worse, and ripening thus for their several dooms. Some we behold working out their lives into greater clearness and nobleness, making steps of their dead selves by which they are mounting to higher and better things. Summoned to the more stern and serious business of life, or brought into the school of adversity, we see them taking shame to themselves that they have played the truant hitherto, learning to look at life as something more than a jest, girding themselves in earnest to its tasks and toil, and leaving for ever behind them the frivolity and the vanity. it may be the folly and the sin, in which hitherto their years were spent. There is no dearer argument with Shakespeare than this, nor one to which he oftener returns. And then, on the other side, he shows us them who will not use aright the discipline of life, who welcome and allow those downward-dragging temptations which beset us all; these waxing worse and worse, forfeiting what good they once possessed, strengthening in their evil, and falling from one wickedness to another. He shows us a Macbeth, met in that most dangerous hour, the hour of his success, giving place to the Devil, allowing the wicked suggestion of the Evil One room in his heart. Then follows the dread concatenation of crime, one ever drawing on, and in a manner rendering necessary, another, till the end is desolation and despair, the blackness of darkness for ever. Where, I sometimes ask myself as I read, where is there a sermon on the need of resisting temptations at the outset, of treading out these sparks of hell before they have set on fire the whole course of nature, like that?

And then, once more: to speak not of what Shakespeare has written, but what Shakespeare was: assuredly we owe him much for the connexion which he has shewn may exist between the loftiest genius and the most perfect sober-mindedness. He had for ever rendered absurd the notion that genius is of necessity irregular, unable to acquiesce in the ordinary conditions of human existence, or cheerfully to adapt itself to these. Doubtless it has often failed in this. There are too many to whom, whether by their own fault, or by some mysterious destiny, the very gifts of heaven have been fatal. The shore of human life is strewn with no sadder wrecks than some which these have made; and not without abundant warrant did a poet of our own age sum up the lives of many who had gone before him, 'the mighty poets *in their misery dead.*' Yes, mighty, but not the mightiest of all. He who towers above every other is memorable in all which we know about him for the even balance of all his faculties; for the equable and harmonious development of his whole being; for the unpretending simplicity which would not allow him to claim any exemptions, any immunities on the score of genius for himself. In nothing eccentric, in nothing differing to the common eye from any other burgher of your town, he bought and sold in your streets; portioned his daughters; invested in prudent purchases the fruits of honourable toil; what he had thus fairly earned he was prepared, if occasion required, to defend by such just help as the law afforded; shrank from no humblest duty of every-day life; and yet all the while knew himself, for he must have known it, the dear heir of a memory which the world should never let die.

You will be asked, before you leave this church to-day, to contribute to the restoring and beautifying of its chancel, in which the dust of Shakespeare, for it is even so near to us, mingles with the common clay. I will only ask you each to imagine to himself this England of ours without her Shakespeare; an England in which he had never lived nor sung. What a crown would be stricken from her brow! How would she come down from the pre-eminence of her place as nursing mother of the foremost poet whom the world has seen, whom, we are almost bold to prophesy, it ever will see! Think how much poorer intellectually, yea, and morally, every one of us would be; what would have to be withdrawn from circulation, of wisest sayings, of profoundest maxims of life-wisdom, which have now been absorbed into the very tissue of our hearts and minds! what regions of our fancy, peopled now with marvellous shapes of strength, of grace, of beauty, of dignity, with beings which have far more reality for us than most of those whom we meet in our daily walk, would be empty and depopulated! And remember that this which we speak of would not be our loss alone, nor the loss of those who have lived already, but the disappearance as well of all that delight, of all that instruction, which, so long as the world endures, he will diffuse in circles ever larger, as the recognition of him in his unapproachable greatness becomes every day more unquestioned, as he moves in the ages which are yet to come 'through ever wider avenues of fame.'

But of this enough. Cease we from man. Let no word be uttered here, which shall even seem to imply that the praise and honour, the admiration and homage, which a man may receive from his fellows are, or can be, the best, the crowning glory of life. Good they are; but they are not the best. Few, in the very nature of things, can be those illustrious sons of memory, dwelling apart from their fellows on the mountain peaks of their solitary grandeur, and dominating from these their own age, and the ages to come. To very few it can be granted, that their names should resound through the centuries, that men shall make long pilgrimages to the place of their birth, gather up the smallest notices of them as infinitely precious, chide an incurious age which suffered so much about them, that would have been priceless to us, to perish for ever, or celebrate with secular solemnities the returning period of their birth.

All this must be the heritage of the fewest; but because such, it cannot be the best of all; for a righteous God would never have put his best and fairest beyond the reach of well-nigh all among his children. This is not the best. That is the best, which all may make their own, those with the smallest gifts as certainly as those with the greatest;—faithfully to fulfil humble duties; to follow Christ, it may be by lowliest paths, unseen of men, though seen of angels and approved of God; and so to have names written not on earth, but in heaven, not on the rolls of earthly fame, but in the Lamb's book of life. For, brethren beloved, I should be untrue to that solemn trust which I bear, untrue to those responsibilities from which I can never divest myself, if I did not remind you, above all if I did not remind you on such a day as this, that goodness is more than greatness, and grace than gifts; that men attain to heaven not soaring on the wings of genius, but patiently climbing by steep stairs of faith and love and obedience; that the brightest crowns, if all their brightness is of earth and none from heaven, are doomed to wither; that there is but one amaranthine crown, even that which Christ gives to them, be they high or low, wise or simple, emperors or clowns, who have loved, and served, and obeyed Him.

This crown they have obtained, the serious and sage poets who have consecrated their divine faculty to the service of Him who lent it. For myself, I am strong to believe that from one so gentle, so tender, so just, so true, as was Shakespeare, the grace to make this highest consecration was not withholden; that we have a right to number him with Dante, with Spenser, with Milton, and with all that august company of poets

'Who sing, and singing in their glory move.'

His intimate, in some sense his profound, acquaintance with Scripture, no one can deny, or the strong grasp which he had of its central truths. He knew the deep corruption of our fallen nature, the desperate wickedness of the heart of man; else he would never have put into the mouth of a prince of stainless life such a confession as this: 'I am myself indifferent honest, but yet I could accuse me of such things that it were better my mother had not borne me, . . . with more offences at my beck than I have thoughts to put them in, imagination to give them shape, or time to act them in.' He has set forth the scheme of our redemption in words as lovely and as exquisite as have ever flowed from the lips of uninspired man :—

'Why, all the souls that were were forfeit once;
And He that might the vantage best have took,
Found out the remedy.'

He has put home to the holiest here their need of an infinite forgiveness from Him who requires truth in the inward parts :—

> 'How would you be,
> If He, which is the top of judgment, should
> But judge you as you are?'

He was one who was well aware what a stewardship was his own in those marvellous gifts which had been entrusted to him, for he has himself told us,

> 'Heaven does with us as we with torches do,
> Not light them for themselves; for if our virtues
> Did not go forth of us, 'twere all alike
> As if we had them not.'

And again he has told us that

> 'spirits are not finely touched
> But to fine issues;'

assuredly not ignorant how finely his own had been touched, and what would be demanded from him in return. He was one who certainly knew that there is none so wise that he can 'circumvent God'; and that for a man, whether he be called early or late,

> 'Ripeness is all.'

Who shall persuade us that he abode outside of that holy temple of our faith, whereof he has uttered such glorious things, admiring its beauty, but not himself entering to worship there? One so real, so truthful, as all which we learn about Shakespeare declares him to have been, assuredly fell in with no idle form of words, when in that last testament which he dictated so shortly before his death, he first of all, and before all, commended his soul to God his Creator; and this (I quote his express words), 'hoping and assuredly believing through the only merits of Jesus Christ my Saviour to be made partaker of life everlasting.' May God grant this to us all.

SERMON XV.

ON THE HEARING OF PRAYER.

JOHN xvi. 23, 24.

Verily, verily, I say unto you, Whatsoever ye shall ask the Father in my name, he will give it you. Hitherto have ye asked nothing in my name: ask, and ye shall receive, that your joy may be full.

THE Church, on this Rogation Sunday, is still in an attitude of waiting, still seeking and asking, as that name implies, the promise of the Father, the Pentecostal gift of the Holy Ghost, who should abide with her for evermore. This Sunday then, which we have reached in our Christian Year, and the Gospel which is appointed for it, from which my text is drawn, will naturally lead us to the subject of prayer, as that which will best befit the day. The subject is eminently in season now, even as it can never be out of season at any time. He who knew what was in man, knew the backwardness to prayer which is in the heart of every one of us; and this, notwithstanding all the present rewards, all the present delights, which it often brings with it; He knew that we needed every motive, every argument to be brought to bear upon us, which might prompt us to a due and diligent performance of this excellent duty. It is for this reason that his Word is so full of goads and incentives to prayer. Now we have Christ, our great exemplar, set before us as Himself praying, rising up a great while before day, and retiring into a solitary place for prayer; and this his prayer no make-believe, but with strong crying and tears. Now He speaks a parable to us that men ought always to pray, and not to faint;[1] now He shews us a Peter delivered from Herod's sword by the prayer made without ceasing of the Church for him;[2] or again, as in the verses before us, He pledges his faithfulness and truth to us that *our* prayers shall be answered, that whatsoever we ask the Father in his name, He will give it; and then, mingling in his own gracious manner command and promise together, He goes on to say, 'Ask, and ye shall receive, that your joy may be full.'

Let us then, my brethren, a little consider,

1st, What it is to ask in the name of Christ.

2ndly, With what necessary limitations, which, though unuttered, must yet be understood, the promise is to be taken, that what we ask we shall receive.

And 3rdly, What the blessed fruit of asking and receiving will be; namely, that our joy will be full.

[1] Luke xviii. 1.   [2] Acts xii. 5–7.

And first, 'Whatsoever ye shall ask the Father in my name, He will give it you.' What is it to ask in the name of Christ? Plainly it must mean a great deal more than merely the closing of each of our prayers and petitions with a certain form of words, as that we ask all for Christ's sake. To ask in the name of Christ is to ask as those who know themselves to have been set by God's grace in the kingdom of the reconciled and the redeemed; as those who have been brought near to the Father by the Son, and who could not, and who continually confess that they could not, have been brought near in any other way. To ask in the name of Christ is to plead his merits, to make mention of his righteousness; to shelter ourselves and all our own sin and guilt and shame behind this righteousness of his; to acknowledge with our lips, to confess with our hearts, that by a sinful nature and by an evil practice we are heirs of shame, children of wrath, less than the least of God's mercies; that we could make no claim to the very smallest of these, but only to indignation and wrath, and to God's extreme malediction which is against all sin, if Christ had not died, if Christ had not risen again, died for our sins, risen again for our justification; if Christ had not ascended to the right hand of the Father; if He were not there even now, our Mediator, our Intercessor, our Advocate, our High Priest. This it is to ask in the Son's name; no cold and heartless formality of the lips, but a deep conviction, modifying, moulding, pervading, colouring all our prayers, that in Christ, and only in Christ, God is perfectly well pleased; and in us only so far as we are found in Him; that all our acceptance with God, all our right to be heard by God, rests solely and exclusively on the work for sinners which Christ once accomplished on Calvary, and is evermore pleading in heaven.

But secondly, we have the promise, 'Whatsoever ye shall ask the Father in my name, He will give it you.' But is this the fact? Does this come true in our actual life? Is not the promise here bigger than the actual fulfilment of the promise in our own experience, or in the experience of others? Questions such as these, not unmixed with misgivings, have probably, at one time or another, passed through and perplexed the minds of us all. But take the words with such limitations as, though not expressed, must plainly be supplied, and there will be found no exaggeration in the promise; nothing to which the experience of God's saints cannot set its seal. Some limitation these words, in the very necessity of things, must receive. Plainly Christ does not pledge Himself here that his Father will give things harmful to his children, even though they in their blindness and shortsightedness should ask such at his hands. To his enemies He may grant their desires, and in the very granting plague them more than if they had been disappointed of their lust. They may seek, like murmuring Israelites, their quails, and may obtain them, may eat and be well filled, and perish while the meat is yet in their mouths.[1] They may ask to be permitted, like Balaam, to go on some errand of covetousness and wrong, and they may be permitted in God's very anger to go, so rushing headlong on their doom. Like the people of Gadara, they may beseech the Lord to depart out of their coasts; and He may take them at their word and leave them, and they may see his face again no more.[2] But with other counsels and by other methods He deals with his own. They too may ask amiss; for there is much of dark, much of carnal in them still. They too may ask that which, if He were to grant, they could not bear; that which would puff them up, which would lead them far away from the paths of their true blessedness, which in one shape or another would be their harm, perhaps their ruin; and this He no more grants them, however eagerly, however passionately they may demand it, than a loving mother would give the red berries of the poisonous nightshade to a wayward and fretful child, even though it should stretch out its eager hands with crying and tears for the deadly boon. There is no pledge then here that God will give any but good things to his children.

[1] Ps. lxxviii. 29–31.   [2] Mark v. 17.

Other things in very faithfulness and love He must withhold, however they may be almost tempted to accuse Him for this that his promise has failed.

But, again, there is no pledge in these words, that God will give to his children what they ask exactly in the form, shape, and manner in which they ask it, even though the thing itself be according to his will. Here, too, they must trust in Him, trust in a Father's love; be sure that He will grant them their desires either in the shape in which they present these to Him, or in a better shape, with some higher and completer fulfilment than it has entered into their thoughts to conceive. Strange, wonderful, mysterious, are the ways in which God answers the prayers of his people. Well for us that we do not always know *how* He will answer them; else, I believe, many a prayer would die upon our lips, and we should not venture to offer it. We ask one thing, and He appears to give us quite another; leads none in the path by which they fain would go; seems to baffle, defeat, disappoint those whom He loves the best; and yet all the while He is the Faithful and the True, is fulfilling the desires of them that fear Him. For what is the desire in which for them all other desires are summed up? Is it not first and chiefly that they may be holy, that they may be among those who shall see his face with joy, and stand without fault before his throne for ever? If such be their prayer of prayers, can any dealing, any discipline of God's, which helps, furthers, sets forward this, be other than an answer to prayer? Like the sons of Zebedee they sue for places in his kingdom, places near to Him, for they love Him; but, short-sighted as they are, anticipating that, in some brief and compendious manner, that kingdom shall be theirs; and little guessing of the cup which they must drink, and the baptism with which they must be baptized, before ever that kingdom can be indeed their own.[1] But, asking the end, He counts that they have also asked the means. Asking holiness, He counts that they have asked all without which that holiness would never have been attained. Asking to be near Him, He counts that they asked each one of the painful and toilsome steps by which the heavenly heights can be scaled, and that nearness won.

They would not have dared explicitly to seek this discipline for themselves. Flesh and blood would have shrunk back from such a prayer; but implicitly they did ask it, even the cup of purifying sorrow, the baptism of cleansing pain; and He, in whose love there is no weakness, who means that his own shall praise Him, not for an hour here, but for an eternity in heaven, listens to the central desire of their hearts, the deepest voice of their souls, which is for holiness; gives them what they asked, though He does not give it to them as they asked

---

[1] Matt. xx. 20.

it. Their beloved, the desire of their eyes, go forth to distant lands, and they pray that they may yet see their faces again in the flesh. They see them not here again; but He gives them blessed assurances that they shall yet behold them once more in heaven. Or they would fain have walked by smooth paths, and in company with one beloved partner of their life, to the City of the heavenly rest; and they have asked that such paths, and in such companionship, might be appointed for their treading. Little by little He makes them to understand that it is by other roads, in loneliness, perhaps, and solitude, and walking, it may be, in the shadow of some life-long grief, that the rest of the heavenly City shall be won. But still, as that was the central and cardinal longing of their hearts, to stand within those diamond walls, to see there the King in his beauty, He is faithful to every jot and tittle of his promise, so long as He makes all things for them work together to this their highest blessedness, and consummation, and joy.

So much, dear friends, to vindicate the faithfulness of God, when He answers prayer in other ways than those which beforehand we have laid down to ourselves, and would fain lay down to Him. Yet it is not meant by this that there is not many a prayer which receives its direct and simple answer; and this in the very form in which it was laid out before his throne; and many more which would do the same, if only they fulfilled the one condition which Christ has imposed on our prayers: 'Whatsoever things ye desire, when ye pray believe that ye receive them, and ye shall have them.' But how hard it is thus to believe. It is comparatively easy to pray—to regard prayer as a healthy, elevating, purifying exercise of the soul; which must have a reactive influence for good on our hearts and our affections; but to regard it as indeed a speaking with God, such a speaking with God as must be followed by a speaking of his to us in return, to follow our prayers with the eye of faith, nothing doubting that they will come back to us in the shape of the strength, the grace, the blessing we have sought for, this we find most hard; sometimes we do not so much as attempt to do it. Take an evidence of the slowness to this which the Church, while yet in the warmth of its first love and earnestness of its first faith, supplied. Peter was in prison, in the dungeon of Herod, appointed to death. 'Prayer,' we are told, 'was made of the Church without ceasing unto God for him;' to wit, that he might be delivered from the sword of Herod and from all the expectation of the Jews. But when this prayer of the Church had been duly heard, and an angel had stricken off the chains from the Apostle's hands, and the doors of his prison had opened of their own accord, and he came, a free man, to those who were in the very act of praying that he might be delivered, that he might be set free, they would not believe it, said it was his angel, affirmed that the maid was mad who brought them the assurance that their prayers had been heard, and that what they sought had been granted indeed.[1] And we, my brethren, are just as slow, or slower, to believe than they were; slow above all to believe in this mystery of prayer, a mystery hidden very often from the wise and prudent, but revealed unto babes. For what is it we need, to enter into this mystery? Surely it is that of which we have so little; it is the child's heart, the belief of the child in its Father's love, and that He will withhold from it no manner of thing which is good.

If, then, you would obtain, ask, expecting to obtain. Launch forth the arrows of your prayer, not as into vacant air and empty space; but let the very throne of God be the mark and scope which you aim at; follow them, these wondrous arrows which, winged by faith, can pierce even heaven; follow them with the eye of faith till they have alighted there; and then expect in one shape or another to hear of them again. He that made the ear, shall He not hear? He into whose own ear there ascend from this earth of ours so many vain, so many proud, so many wanton, so many cruel, so many blasphemous words, the harsh grating discords of

[1] Acts xii. 16.

sinful earth, shall He not hear the sighing of contrite hearts, the voices of faithful supplication, the appeals of children to their Father's love; these which are the harmonies no less of heaven than of earth, as sweet or sweeter than the hallelujahs of angels to Him that sitteth upon the throne?

Having, then, such promises as these, see, I beseech you, to this matter of prayer, to which such precious promises are linked. Other arguments I might use. I might remind you, and your own experience would set a seal to my words, that it is the very breath of your spiritual life, that without which this life will pine, wither, and die. And if there be any here to-day who have yet to learn this, I cannot refrain from saying, and that with all the plainness of speech which our office as ambassadors of Christ imposes, which the vital importance of the subject demands,—whatever decencies of a religious life you may be maintaining before the world, whatever fair show of a religious profession you may be making before the Church, yet if you be living without earnest constant prayer, prayer which is prayer indeed, a pressing out of your own darkness into God's marvellous light, a laying hold of his strength in your own utter weakness, you are living without God in the world; and therefore knowing nothing of those mighty transforming powers, powers of the world to come, which are evermore at work in his Church, changing those who submit themselves to them, from carnal to spiritual, from earthly to heavenly, from children of this world to children of the living God.

Ask, then, I beseech you, one and all, that so you may receive, and that your joy may be full; not scanty, as now even for the best of us it too often is, but abundant; not intermittent, but continuous and unfailing; that, so receiving, you may not be poor, when such riches, riches of grace and strength, may be yours for the asking; that you may not be sick, with all the means of health within your reach; but may by your own experience make proof that, when God gave to his children prayer, He gave them the golden key which unlocks the treasure-house of heaven, bade them, so to speak, to help themselves; said to them, and said not in vain, that all things were theirs.

SERMON XVI.[1]

THE KINGDOM WHICH COMETH NOT WITH OBSERVATION.

LUKE xvii. 20.

The kingdom of God cometh not with observation.

WE have here the proclamation of a law which holds good, not merely in the kingdom of heaven, that kingdom of divine operations, but one which, with only few and partial exceptions, holds good no less in every region of human activity; for it is not merely this Church of the living God, the mightiest and most marvellous birth which the world has ever seen, that 'cometh not with observation'; but of every great movement, great event, great institution, of all in short, or of well nigh all, which has exercised a deep and lasting influence on the after-history of the world, it may be noted that it has had small and unobserved beginnings, has grown up like the mustard seed, without observation; while loud and grand commencements, summoning as with the sound of a trumpet the whole world to behold what a mighty birth is at hand,

[1] Preached on Whitsunday.

or what a glorious thing has just been born; these are almost sure to come to nothing, to end in shameful discomfiture and defeat. Thus, who has ever traced the obscure rudiments, the first foundations of that wondrous city on the banks of the Tiber, which was for so many centuries queen and mistress of the world; and which, when the sceptre of temporal sovereignty dropped from her aged hand, presently grew young again, and wielded, as with a new lease of life and of power, a spiritual dominion more wide and wonderful than ever her temporal had been? Who knows the secrets of the birth of Rome? But who does *not* know with how loud a promise, with how vainglorious an announcement, an older city was proposed to be built, the city and the tower whose top should reach unto heaven; what a name and a fame its builders designed beforehand for themselves, organizing, as they were purposed to do, into one grand society all the tribes and families of the earth;[1] and how, in a little while, nothing but a deformed and shapeless mass of bricks remained to tell of the city which should have been at once the symbol and the centre of their world-wide sovereignty and dominion?

And this silent coming of whatever shall prove great indeed, true in many regions of human activity, is truest of all in that highest region of all, where human

[1] Gen. xi. 4.

and divine most work together. 'It is the glory of God to conceal a matter.' If other momentous births 'come not with observation,' with pomp and circumstance and pride, challenging notice, noised abroad by the thousand tongues of rumour and report, least of all does the kingdom of God come with these. And for the confirming of this assertion, what history so wonderful as that of this kingdom's first coming; of the exaltation, within three centuries after its first planting, of the Church of Christ upon the high places of the earth? By what silent courses, by what unmarked degrees, by what invisible agencies did that new life, whereof the Son of God was the Author and Giver, impart of itself to an old and dying world; working its way from within to without, from below to above, from the centre to the circumference; gradually transmuting, transforming, and transfiguring whatever was brought into contact with it? How little did that proud heathen world, how little did imperial Rome, throned in her golden palaces, amusing herself in her bloody amphitheatres, dream that she nourished within her bosom a mightier than herself, a weakness which would be stronger than all her strength, a foolishness which should be wiser than all her wisdom, a patience which should weary out all her cruelty, a love which should vanquish all her hate. To one seeing but as man sees, where was there ever a strength, a splendour, a glory like hers, the fourth beast which Daniel saw, 'dreadful and terrible, and strong exceedingly,' whose iron teeth had broken in pieces all the kingdoms of the earth, and was stamping the residue of them beneath its feet?[1] And where, on the other hand, was a weakness like theirs, the votaries, in the judgment of one of the wisest and most tolerant among the heathen, of 'an exaggerated and detestable superstition;' followers 'of one Jesus, which was dead,' whom somewhere in Syria a Roman governor had once put to death, but whom these obstinate and perverse enthusiasts 'affirmed to be still alive'?

What could be the issue of a conflict between opposing forces so unequally matched as these? What credit would he have found, who in the second, yes, and far on into the third century, had announced to the princes of this world, the leaders of its thought, the wielders of its power, to Roman senator or Greek philosopher, that the future was not with them; that it had passed out of their hands; that it belonged to the adherents of this despised Oriental superstition? Would they have believed him, if he had told them that the palace of their Cæsars itself, not to speak of their own households, was already filled with the votaries of it; that the very ground beneath their feet was honeycombed with the long galleries wherein were laid thousands and tens of thousands who had already lived and

[1] Dan. vii. 7,

died in the faith of this crucified Man; nay, that the hour was coming, was even at the door, when Rome herself, in the person of the highest representative of her majesty and her power, should worship before Him, and should confess to Him as Lord of lords and King of kings?

Strange, incredible announcement! and yet, as we know, true notwithstanding. The leaven wrought. The mustard seed grew. The stone cut out without hands became a great mountain, and filled the whole earth.[1] The waters which issued from the sanctuary, reaching to the ankles at first, were anon to the knees, and then presently to the loins, and ere long waters to swim in, a river that could not be passed over;[2] while yet all this, attracting slightest notice, coming unobserved, unawares overtook a world which little knew what and how great blessings were about to break forth upon it; the kingdom only revealing itself for what it was, when all the preparations for it were consummated and completed.

But this, my brethren, which is thus true of the kingdom as a whole, shows itself also true continually of that same kingdom as it severally comes to one and another who receives it. I do not deny that it comes sometimes and to some souls as in the storm and in the earthquake, in mighty shakings for them as of the earth

---

[1] Dan. ii. 34, 35.   [2] Ezek. xlvii. 1–5.

and of the heaven ; but more often far in the still small
voice, finding its way by secret invisible channels, such
as it fashions for itself, into the hearts of men; changing everything, and in the end glorifying everything;
and yet all the while working unseen, its operations
withdrawn from the world's eyes, nay, sometimes, and
for a while almost withdrawn from the knowledge of
them over whom this mighty change is passing.

And if you ask the reason of this, that reason is not
far to seek. These are its actings, because it is the
kingdom of the Spirit; of that Spirit which was, as upon
this day, poured out on all flesh ; on all, that is, who do
not resist and close their hearts against it, on as many
as the Lord God shall call ; this kingdom therefore being
round us and about us, as truly round and about our spirits
as the air is round and about our bodies, sustaining *them*
by that equable pressure which it exerts on every side;
being, as it is, the element by which those bodies live,
inhaled and again exhaled at every breath which we
draw. Even so fares it with this kingdom of the Spirit,
encompassing every one of us like a spiritual atmosphere; where it has not entered, seeking to enter;
fashioning ways of entrance for itself; standing at the
door and knocking; and never content till it constitutes
itself a kingdom of God within us, and not merely one
round about us. For, indeed, this is the meaning of
all the discipline of our lives, of the joy and the sorrow,

of the honour and the dishonour, of the health and the sickness, of those days when God has seemed to make a hedge about us and ours, so that no evil has come nigh our dwelling; and of those other days when, it may be, He has broken forth upon us, breach upon breach, and the grave has said 'Give, give,' and take our choicest and our best. What, I say, is the meaning of all this, of the height and the depth, the joy and the sorrow, the chances and changes innumerable of our mortal life; nor to speak of more intimate and mysterious dealings of God with our spirits; what but that by one admonishment or another, in answer to this knocking or to that, we might open to Him the door, and, He entering in, the knigdom might be indeed within us, and we, in the highest and most blessed sense of all, in the kingdom?

No more is needed for this than the act of our faith, that we believe and receive that, as on this day, the last, highest, and most abiding gift of God to his creatures, a gift implied in the creation and constitution of man, but one which could not be actually conferred in its fulness and universality, until Christ had glorified the nature of man at the right hand of the Father; that, as on this day, this gift was imparted, this kingdom of the Spirit founded. For so it is; and thenceforward that poor mean weary world which our natural eyes behold, and in which our natural lives are spent, is not all; that world of getting and spending, of rising up to toil and lying down for weariness, of pushing and striving, of one losing and another winning, with all its innumerable meannesses and falsehoods is not all. Beside it and behind it, too often hidden for us by it, there is another world; I do not mean a world very far off, such as we may hope to reach by and bye, in another state of existence, but one in which we may be living and moving even now, in which tens of thousands are living and moving at this moment, a world, or call it rather a kingdom, of righteousness and peace and joy in the Holy Ghost. It is one which can take all the meanness, the weariness, and the dreariness, and the vanity out of that other world; or if it leave ought of these, leaving only enough to make us yearn and cry for a still more perfect deliverance; while in this taking, incomplete though it may be, a pledge is given us, that these shall one day disappear altogether, and the shadows give place to substance, and the emptiness to fulness, and the falsehoods to realities, and the weariness to perfect rest, and the meanness and mutability to the glory, dignity, and honour of that kingdom, which knows no change, even as it knows no sin.

Yes, dear friends, such a kingdom not merely will be, but *is*. Our eyes may be holden, and we may not see it; God may be in this place, and we may not know it. Our waking dreams may be of far other things than those shining stairs which connect heaven and earth, with angels ascending and descending by them on the Son of Man; but as our faith does not first create these blessed and transcendent facts, so as little does our unbelief do away with them or destroy them. That kingdom cannot deny itself; though, alas! we may only too easily deny our part and portion in it.

I have spoken of it mainly, and to this I have been naturally led by the festival of this day, as the kingdom of the Spirit; and yet when I remind you of that share in this kingdom which every one among us may claim, I am myself reminded that I should not omit further to remind you that the Spirit who was as upon this day given is the Spirit of the Father and of the Son; and the kingdom which was as upon this day founded, the kingdom of the Father and of the Son. There can be nothing more dangerous, as past experience has abundantly shown, than to separate, even in thought, the gift of to-day from the work of Good Friday, of the Easter morning, of the Ascension Day. It is because the Son of God has died for our sins, and risen again for our justification, and having ascended, has sat down on the right hand of the Majesty on high, it is therefore that this Spirit is given, even as a pure river of water of life, clear as crystal, proceeding out of the throne of God and of the Lamb; in other words, as the Spirit of the Father and the Son. Know Him as such;

no mere vague floating influence, but a personal Spirit, as truly a Person as the other Persons of the ever-blessed Trinity; so manifold and so mighty in his operations, that the seven lamps of fire burning before the throne are declared to be the seven spirits of this one Spirit, the sevenfold mighty workings of the same; even as you heard this morning, that it was in tongues of divided flame He first descended on the Church. As light, that is, and as fire; as light to illumine, light to make manifest all the hidden things of our darkness; as fire to warm, and also to consume; yes, blessed be God, as fire to consume, to burn up the chaff with unquenchable fire; for when we think, dear friends, of all the chaff, the straw, the stubble, the dross in ourselves, shall we not thank God that this Spirit is fire, and, whatever else He may consume or spare, and on that awful question I enter not now, pledged to burn up all this with unquenchable fire?

For the rest, let Him come in this way or in that, with observation or without it; only see that in whatever shape He comes and his kingdom comes, you welcome and receive Him. The wind bloweth where it listeth. If only it be filling the sails of thy soul, it matters not so much to thee whence it cometh; nor, if only it be bearing thee heavenward, whither it goeth. If only thou findest thyself in the kingdom of the Spirit, that Spirit teaching, that Spirit guiding, that Spirit enlightening, that Spirit sanctifying, ask not too curiously by what steps thou camest thither.

It is blessedness enough, and more than enough, to be there; for that kingdom to which thou belongest may be a hidden one now, grudgingly acknowledged, or not acknowledged at all, by the wise and prudent of this world, and thou a hidden one in that kingdom; yet of this be sure, that, however without observation now, it will in the end be the observed of all observers, the admired of all admirers, the cynosure of every eye, the one glory when every other glory shall have paled; the one name and fame which shall survive when every other shall have passed away as a noise; the one kingdom which, itself immovable, shall behold the wreck and the ruin of every kingdom besides; and then, in that kingdom of the Spirit, that kingdom of the truth, wherein goodness shall be the only measure of greatness, and each and all shall wear an outward beauty exactly corresponding to the inward beauty of the Christ which shall be formed in them; or, alas! shall put on an outward deformity corresponding to the inner unloveliness of their hearts and lives; then, I say, in that kingdom of the truth, all that are of the truth, and thou, if thou art of this, shall shine out as the sun in the kingdom of their Father, for Christ, who is their life, shall have appeared, and they too shall appear with Him in glory.

SERMON XVII.

PRESSING TOWARD THE MARK.

Phil. iii. 12.

Not as though I had already attained.

How wonderful is this language on the lips of St. Paul, —that he, after so many years of discipleship, after so many years of apostleship, should still be striving, still pressing forward, should still feel how far short of the goal he was; and forgetting the things which were behind, should reach forward still to those which were before; with all his knowledge of Christ, counting that there was a knowledge of Him, higher, deeper, larger, fuller than any to which he had yet attained, that there was a power of Christ and of his resurrection which as yet he had not known, but which it was possible for him to know. And if this language is wonderful on the lips of the Apostle, there must in Christ be a wonder corresponding. What, we may fitly ask, must be the glory, beauty, and excellency of that Lord whom St. Paul for so many years had served; when he, the great Apostle himself, had only caught some glimpses of these? What must be the power of Christ in them that believe, when he had hitherto known this power only in part? You remember, perhaps, how the mightiest discoverer in natural science of modern times, I mean Sir Isaac Newton, said toward the close of his life, that he was but as a child, who had gathered a few shells on the shores of an illimitable sea. He saw stretching before him a vast ocean of knowledge, which his life had been too short, which even *his* powers had been too weak, to explore. What *he* felt in things natural, St. Paul felt in things spiritual,—that there were heights above him which he had never scaled, depths beneath him which he had never fathomed; that, rich as he was in Christ, there were yet hidden in that Lord treasures of wisdom and knowledge which would make him far richer still; that God was unsearchable, unfathomable, a shoreless sea, an ocean of perfections; of which he understood a little, of which he was understanding ever something more; but which man could no more take in than he could hold the sea and all its multitudinous waves in the hollow of his hand. Skirts of his glory St. Paul had seen, but not his train which filled the temple of the universe. Secrets of Christ's power he had known, who in this very Epistle declared, 'I can do *all things* through Christ which strengtheneth me;' and yet he felt that there was a power of Christ, transcending all which

even he had known; and like some great earthly
conqueror, who should esteem nothing won while anything remained to win, nothing accomplished while
anything was yet possible to accomplish; who slighted,
despised, trampled under foot all his old successes in
the eager pursuit of new; even so this mighty spiritual
athlete, this captain, commander, conqueror, leader of
the hosts of the Lord, could not stay his steps, could
not arrest his course. For himself, and for those whom
he had hitherto led from victory to victory, he was
still covetous of more; more victory over sin, more
triumphs over the world, more casting down of the
strongholds of Satan, more spoiling of principalities and
powers; to be more clothed with humility, to follow
after a more perfect holiness, to know more of that
love of Christ which passes knowledge.

I have thought, dear friends, that we might all be
fitly reminded what on these matters was the mind of
Paul; how little he, this eminent servant of God, was
content with any attainments which he had already
made; because it is not to be denied that there is much
continually tempting every one of us to stand still, to
acquiesce and rest satisfied in that whereunto we have
attained, instead of pressing forward to the things which
are before. How often do we see those in the Church
of Christ, who appear to take for granted that there is
to be one, and one only, serious struggle for them in the

whole course of their spiritual existence, the passage, so to speak, from darkness to light, from death to life. But this conflict over, this passage successfully accomplished, being thus 'converted,' they appear also to take for granted that no other conflict deserving the name remains for them. This struggle is for them like the difficult passage over the breakers at the bar of a river; which if once prosperously accomplished, the ship is henceforward in smooth water, in a safe harbour, and may lay its account so to continue to the end. But is it so? Can it be truly affirmed that all the serious difficulties and dangers of the Christian life are at the outset? Doubtless, that is a tremendous crisis in every man's spiritual life, when he first wakes up to the knowledge of sin; and despite of all its agonies and its terrors a blessed crisis, if only hand in hand with this knowledge of sin goes the knowledge of Christ the forgiver of sin, whose blood cleanses from its stain, whose spirit delivers from its dominion. But serious, solemn, awful, yea terrible as this sometimes is, blessed as the victory is of him who by faith beholds his sin put away, and himself reconciled with God, causing as it does angels to sing their *Te Deums* in heaven, still this is not all; and it is a mistake most dangerous to ourselves, most dishonouring to our God, if we count it all; if we be content to remain victors in this first battlefield, to hold what we have then and there won, to make that the goal which was only the starting-place, that the Omega which was only the Alpha of the life which we should have lived in Christ. So acting, we should only too much resemble the children of Israel; we should act over again their sin, who were content if only they could just make room for themselves in the land which the Lord had given them to possess it wholly; who were at no pains to drive out the Canaanites; but came to terms of dishonourable accommodation with those whom they should have thoroughly rooted out from the land.[1]

This course, as I said just now, is at once most dangerous to ourselves, and most dishonouring to our God. I will dwell on both these points a little. It is most dangerous to ourselves. I urge this the first, being as it is the poorer and lower motive, and preferring to reserve the higher and nobler to the last. He who resolves that he will stand still, is making sure for himself, though he may not think it or intend it, that he will go back. Not to grow is to decay. It is only by a series of new efforts, new starts, as it were, new beginnings, revivings of the work within us, that we so much as keep our place, and manage not to lose the ground which we have already made our own. We find the motive to these new starts now in some searching discourse, now in some holy book, now in the word, now in the example, of some more advanced Christian friend;

[1] Judg. i. 27–34; ii. 1, 2.

now Christ meets us at his table, making us perhaps to feel that we can only just claim to have the marriage garment of the welcome guests; now it is sickness, now it is sorrow, which does the work appointed for it to accomplish; delivers the message which it was charged to bring; for all these things and a thousand more God works with his children, submitting them to chance and change, emptying them from vessel to vessel, lest they should settle down upon their lees. But if we will not accept the admonishment which all these dealings of his contain, if we will not answer to the call which they make upon us, shall we keep even what we have gotten, shall we remain even where we are? Does the boat which was making difficult headway against a strong current remain where it was, when the rowers idly rest upon their oars? And is the Christian life anything else than such a toilsome struggle against the stress and stream of our own corrupt inclinations? I do not speak now, brethren, of higher rewards, a brighter crown, a more glorious inheritance, a place nearer to the throne, which we may so miss; but I say that our being saved at all is seriously compromised, is brought into imminent danger, unless the motto of St. Paul's life, *Plus ultra*, 'I reach forth unto those things which are before,' is the motto also of ours. Where all is loss, with no compensating gain, where the world is ever at work to abate the edge of our spirits, and no new edge is given.

to them again, what is likely to be the end it is only too easy to imagine.

But I am unwilling to appeal to you solely on such grounds as these, when there are so much higher on which I can rest my appeal. The Gospel of Christ was not given to us only or chiefly that we might be safe. He who reads the question, 'What must I do to be saved?' as though it were asked, 'What shall I do to be safe, to provide for my own personal security?' is bringing selfishness into that scheme, the whole plan and purpose of which was to expel selfishness, and to substitute higher principles of action in its room. I will therefore remind you further that such a course is one most dishonouring to our God. For why was it that He called us out of darkness into his marvellous light? Was it for our sakes merely? or was it not also for the praise and glory of his own name, that we might show forth his praise, that we might be his witnesses, that in us might be seen the exceeding greatness of his power; how of clods of earth He could make stars of heaven, hewing from the rough quarries of earth polished stones for glory and for beauty that should adorn the walls of that spiritual temple which He is building, and shall one day fill with his presence? But if this be the end of our calling, to show forth his praise, to do valiantly in his name, to tread under foot at once his enemies and our own, namely, all the power of the

Evil One, it is clear that this only we shall do as we are growing in grace, as we are passing from the condition of little children, who just know that their sins are forgiven for Christ's name's sake, unto that of young men, who are strong and in whom the word of God abideth, and who have overcome the Wicked One; in due time to be enrolled among those whom St. John addresses as fathers for their ripe experience, and for the fulness of their knowledge of the mystery of Christ.[1]

Brethren beloved, if you ask me how shall we escape a danger which lies so near to every one of us, overcome a temptation which so flatters our indolence, but yet at the same time so entirely defeats the highest purposes for which we were called, which may cause us to make entire shipwreck of our souls, I have no advice to give but the most obvious, no counsels which have not been given ten thousand times before. I can only put you in remembrance of things which you already perfectly know. And yet even this may be profitable; much of our preaching in the very necessity of things must consist of such a putting in remembrance as this.[2]

First, then, let me remind you, how in spiritual things it is just as true as in worldly, that 'the hand of the diligent maketh rich,' while he that dealeth with a

---

[1] 1 John ii. 12–14.   [2] Jude 5; 2 Pet. i. 13.

slack hand is hastening to poverty. Of two who began their Christian life together why does one grow in grace, and the other stand still, or, it may be, rather go backward than forward? We intrude not here into the secrets of God's grace. He may give of his mere freedom larger, freer, more abundant supplies of grace to one than to another; or, even if grace is equal, the soil of one heart may be kindlier for the ripening the fruits of the Spirit than that of another; but yet it stands true in the main and in the long run that this hand of the diligent maketh rich. Devout diligence in prayer, devout diligence in the study of God's Word, devout diligence in waiting on Him at his Holy Table, and in all other means of grace; and last but not least, devout diligence in the outward work of the Lord, these are the helps appointed for you, by aid of which you are to grow in grace and in the love and knowledge of Christ the Lord.

Devout diligence in prayer; here indeed is the mainspring of the whole Christian life. In this we speak with God, and God with us. Of Christ, our pattern and example, we are told that, while He prayed, the fashion of his countenance was altered.[1] All prayer, which truly deserves the name, has in its degree, and exerts on the worshipper, such a transforming, transfiguring power. While he is praying the fashion

[1] Luke ix. 29.

of the countenance of his soul, yes and oftentimes the fashion of his bodily countenance, is altered. In medieval legends of saints we are continually told of holy men that while they prayed they were lifted up from the earth and nearer to heaven. Now this, which of course is not true in the letter, is yet a sort of clumsy, confused expression of the blessed truth, that prayer does in a higher sense lift man from earth toward heaven, infinitely nearer to God than he could otherwise have been. Oh, how careful will you be, as many as mean to press forward, about your times of prayer; outwardly, that they should not be encroached on, that they should not be abridged; inwardly, that they may be times of a real laying hold of God and of his strength. You will lay to heart this solemn truth, that almost all apostasies, all fallings away from God, have begun in the secret chamber. The Demases who have forsaken Paul and Paul's Lord, having loved this present world, there was probably nothing outwardly to distinguish them from the Lukes who were faithful to the end. One tree stood as fair to look at as the other. The only difference was that one had roots and the other had none. When therefore the tempest came, one stood, and the other fell. See that ye be rooted and grounded in Christ. Be very jealous of your times of prayer. Enlarge them, if and when you can. Let nothing but the most absolute necessity persuade you to diminish them.

But once more, he that has that noblest of all ambitions, the ambition which St. Paul expressed in my text, will nourish himself daily and largely on the words of eternal life. Magazines, newspapers, novels, histories, what a thousand competitors there are, seeking to absorb the little leisure which is all that most of us have at our own disposal, to drive the Scriptures into some obscure corner of the day, or to drive them out of the day altogether. How resolute many of us must be if we are to find *any* time for the study of the word of God. And yet it is the *study* of it which we need. It is when we sit under the shadow of this tree of life, and gently shake the branches, then it drops its golden fruit into our lap, not when we hastily pass it by, or gaze on it from afar. Brethren, as many as would grow in grace, by this self-denial or by that win to yourselves some time for this study, not starving your souls of this their necessary food.

Nor less will the Table of the Lord be precious to you, and you frequent guests thereat. Some who have made much progress in the spiritual life have told us that they found signal advantage in bringing each time that they drew nigh to that Holy Table, some special request which they then laid before their Lord. On one occasion it would be, perhaps, that they might obtain perfect victory over some temptation which was grievously harassing them; another time that the Lord would impart to them some grace in which they felt themselves greatly deficient; at another time the special request might be for the conversion of a child, or some other dearly beloved. These are devices in which one will find profit, and another not; yet many, I think, might find their advantage in thus at the Holy Communion gathering the longings and desires of their hearts to a single head, and seeking to carry away some special boon at each of these times of refreshing.

But all this being said, it would be a grievous omission if I did not further and lastly remind you that as many as love the Lord, and would fain love Him more, they labour for the Lord, and would fain labour for Him more. St. Paul pressing toward the mark was no selfish, solitary runner; he sought to draw many with him. The prize of the high calling of God in Christ Jesus would have been no prize to him, if others had not shared it with him. The increase which he desired, which he sought with all his might to set forward, was the increase not of a single limb, but of the whole body to the edifying of itself in love. Let his mind be also ours.

SERMON XVIII.[1]

THE VALLEY OF DRY BONES.

EZEK. xxxvii. 9, 10.

Then said he unto me, Prophesy unto the wind, prophesy, son of man, and say to the wind, Thus saith the Lord God; Come from the four winds, O breath, and breathe upon these slain, that they may live. So I prophesied as he commanded me, and the breath came into them, and they lived, and stood up upon their feet, an exceeding great army.

PERHAPS there is no prophet of the Old Covenant, whose writings offer to us such sublime, original, and sometimes terrible imagery as those of the prophet Ezekiel. What a picture has he drawn and spread out before our eyes in those ten verses, of which you have just heard the concluding. 'The hand of the Lord was upon me, and carried me out in the spirit of the Lord, and set me down in the midst of the valley which was full of bones, and caused me to pass by them round about: and, behold, there were very many in the open valley; and, lo, they were very dry.' The prophet, we gather from

---

[1] Preached on behalf of the Society for the Propagation of the Gospel.

these words, had been carried in the spirit to some ancient battle-plain; some vast fields of blood, of which the world owns now so many; where, in ages long before, two mighty armies had met, and fought, and parted, leaving the earth encumbered with their unburied dead. The flesh of these slain had long since wasted away. The jackal, the wolf, the vulture, the worm, had fed sweetly on it. But bones innumerable, ghastly trophies of death, bleached by the sun and rain and wind, still strewed the ground, and attested the dreadful work which had here been wrought, of the children of Cain who had here met to slaughter and destroy one another.

As the prophet is gazing on this ghastly spectacle, on these bones 'very many and very dry,' the Lord asks him, 'Son of man, can these bones live?' He answers in language not unlike to that of the seer in the Apocalypse,[1] 'O Lord God, thou knowest.' Thou, he would say, canst breathe life into any death; but whether this Thou wilt, is a secret which Thou hast reserved for Thyself. Again the Lord said unto him: , Prophesy unto these dry bones, and say unto them, O ye dry bones, hear the word of the Lord.' Marvellous and stupendous were the results which followed. Listen to them in the prophet's own words: 'So I prophesied as I was commanded: and as I prophesied, there was a

[1] Rev. vii. 14.

noise, and behold a shaking, and the bones came together, bone to his bone. The sinews and the flesh came up upon them, and the skin covered them above: but there was no breath in them'—all the forms of life, but as yet no actual life itself, each bone knit to his bone, the integuments of flesh clothing again the naked skeleton; but thus far no breath, no animating principle of life. 'Then he said unto me, Prophesy unto the wind, prophesy, son of man, and say to the wind, Thus saith the Lord God; Come from the four winds, O breath, and breathe upon these slain, that they may live. So I prophesied as he commanded me, and the breath came into them, and they lived, and stood up upon their feet, an exceeding great army.'

Needs it, O friends, any words of ours to enhance the grandeur, the terror, the magnificence of the picture here presented to your spiritual eye? Needs it any words of ours to explain the inner meaning of this famous vision of the prophet-priest of the Captivity? If we have at all apprehended that meaning, we shall own that this vision of the dry bones, coming first together at the word of the prophet, and then breathed on by the breath of life, and by that quickening breath made to stand upon their feet, and transformed into an army of living men, wonderfully represents to us that work of the Lord which began at Pentecost, when the word of the Lord went forth, and the Spirit of the Lord with that word breathed mercifully and mightily on a dead world, renewed the moral face of the earth, and commenced that wondrous transformation, that regeneration, which having its beginning in the hearts of men, shall not cease till *all* things shall have been made new, a new heaven and a new earth, in which righteousness shall dwell.

For, even while we freely recognise to the full what of glorious and good the heathen world had to show, we still confidently ask, What in its grand sum total was the moral condition of the world till Christ lived and died and rose again, and ascending up on high from thence gave gifts unto men? Have we not a right to say, nay, should we not be compelled to say, that it was in the main even as this valley of dry bones, peopled with men who one to the other seemed alive, went about the tasks, fulfilled the functions, pursued the pleasures of this lower life; but in the eye of God were dead, dead in their trespasses and their sins; that in every part of the world, sin reigned, and death, death moral and spiritual, with sin? Contemplate that world, not as clothed in that false glamour and deceitful splendour with which Art and Poetry invested it, but as it must have presented itself to eyes purer than to behold iniquity; contemplate it, I say, exactly on that Pentecostal day, which we may justly call the birth-day of the Church;—only one small people upon the whole earth preserving the knowledge, the faith, the worship of the true God; and they only using this knowledge to sin more guiltily, because against clearer light and knowledge, than the other nations of the world; their hands still red with the blood of Him whom they should have welcomed as their King and their God;—the rest of the world 'wholly given to idolatry'; and with idolatry to what strange and hideous forms of evil! Contemplate for an instant the gladiatorial shows of Rome, men killing one another to make sport for lookers on; by tens and by hundreds 'butchered to make a Roman holiday.' Contemplate, but with hasty and averted eye, the strange lusts of Greece, men glorying in their shame, and boasting of wickednesses which one would suppose no darkness would have seemed to them thick enough to hide; the world having cast up its Tiberius, as a little later it did its Caligula, its Nero, its Domitian; setting him in the highest place which it had to offer; saying to him, a wretch a thousand times unworthy to live, 'Thou art our *Imperator*, our emperor, our commander; thou art the man whom we delight to honour; to set at the crown of things; in thee we behold the truest image of what we ourselves would fain be, if only we possessed the power.'

Then, when all things were thus at the worst, the Son of God was manifested in the flesh, lived a life of perfect obedience, made on His cross a perfect offering for all the sins, past, present, and to come, of all mankind; rose again, in manifest sign and token that this offering had been accepted, went up on high, and, being exalted at the right hand of God, shed abroad his gifts upon men, even the rebellious. And when they that were ambassadors of his grace, at his bidding began to prophesy, immediately there was a great shaking among the dry bones in the valley of death, everywhere a mighty agitation; life once more was in conflict with death and overcoming death! and as the breath of God passed first over the Jewish Church and then over the Gentile world, and breathed upon those slain, multitudes came up out of their graves, the graves which sin had dug for them,—three thousand souls, we know, on the day of Pentecost, were the first-fruits of a far mightier harvest,—and all stood upon their feet, an exceeding great army of living men, made now by that quickening breath of the Holy Ghost alive unto God. And ever as these messengers of Christ, and such as in succession took up the message from their lips, proclaimed the words of that life, and said in the name and in the power of God, 'Come from the four winds, O breath, and breathe upon these slain,' the same effects followed; the Holy Ghost was given; and multitudes, alienated hitherto from the life of God, dead in their sins, lived to holiness and to God.

Sad, brethren, it is to think that there should have

been ever pause or remission in such a blessed work of re-animation as this. But that such pause or remission has been we cannot deny. Looking out upon the world, as at this present moment it offers itself to our eyes, is not the spectacle which it presents only too like that seen in the visions of God by the prophet of the older Covenant—with indeed this blessed difference, that the valley of the dry bones has never since that day of Pentecostal gifts been wholly a valley of death, wrapt in the utter silence of the grave? The promise has still been made good for those who would believe it, 'Behold, I will cause breath to enter into you, and ye shall live?' the prophesying of the word of the Lord has never ceased; nor yet, as the result of that prophesying, the noise and the shaking, the coming together of the dry bones, and then the animating and quickening of these by the breath of the living God. Death reigns not now everywhere, as once; but yet, oh! how much death, how much that has refused and is still refusing to live. Not to speak of those whom the false religions of the world, Hindoo and Buddhist and Mahommedan, have slain, who go down to the grave with a lie in their right hand, nor yet of the votaries and victims of a thousand meaner superstitions and idolatries, is not Christendom itself a spectacle at this day which well might make angels weep?—which would make *our* heads a fountain of tears if we had that earnest zeal for the glory of God, that true compassion for the perishing souls of men which we ought. For surely the slain in it are many —those whom superstition has slain, and those whom infidelity has slain—the slain by intemperance, and the slain by covetousness, and the slain by uncleanness, and the slain by pride, and by a thousand other weapons of the enemy;—who could number up their multitudes? Pray, brethren, ye who have any feeling sense of what the Church of the living God ought to be, terrible in its ranks as an army with banners, and what it is, resembling as it does only too nearly a valley of dry bones—pray, as did the prophet of old, 'Come from the four winds, O breath of God, and breathe upon these slain, that they may live.' And as prayer is a mockery, unless work is added to it, add in one shape or another your work to your prayers.

But how, if there be among us any to-day whose own condition is only too like that of the dry bones of the valley, any saying in his heart, as said the children of Israel of old, 'Our bones are dried, and our hope is lost; no breath of God shall ever again renew the face of our souls, no life of God shall ever again quicken our dead spirits'? I know how easily such a despair of ourselves may creep over us, and what a covenant with death we seal when we give place to such despair. But have any, I ask, a right to do this, to seal such a covenant as that is—above all, have they a right to do this, when God has given to us such a Scripture as that on which we have been dwelling to-day, or when He permits us in our Christian Year to keep such a festival as Pentecost? For these, why were they *dry* bones, why were they not simply men just dead, the fresh corpses of those newly slain in some battle of yesterday, with the echoes of a life that had hardly departed yet ringing in them, which were thus seen by the prophet in the visions of God to stand up on their feet? Why were they the dry bones of ages past and of battles long ago, which he thus describes as again penetrated by the quickening Spirit from on high? Why but to teach us this, that there are no sinners who have lain so long festering in sin as in the corruption of the tomb, none with habits of evil so ingrained and inveterate, as to be incapable of renewal and revival. He who is the Prince of Life, who has the seven spirits of God, calls, and at his potent voice not merely a daughter of Jairus, who had just expired, or a widow's son as yet unburied, or a Lazarus just four days dead, not merely the sinners of yesterday or the day before, may rise up and walk, alive among the living; but at that almighty bidding those whom sin had slain long ago, so long that now they are out of all hope ever to be otherwise than they are, those also may live again, pierced and penetrated through and through in their dry marrowless bones, until they also stand on their feet once more, part of the army of living men, the soldiers and servants of the living God. Beloved, doubt it not. We perish, because we will not believe in the love, and because we will not believe in the power, of God, in that mighty power of God, able of stones to raise up children to Abraham, mighty to change sinners into saints, clods of earth into stars of heaven, haters of God into lovers of God, persecutors of the faith into preachers of the faith, Sauls into Pauls; to whom no marvels of mercy and of might are impossible.

Is it not even so? You have heard the words of one Seer of the Old Covenant, listen to those of another in the New: 'And he shewed me a pure river of water of life, clear as crystal, proceeding out of the throne of God and of the Lamb.'[1] What is the 'pure river of water of life' but the Holy Ghost given to men, who proceedeth from the Father and from the Son? Turn back again to our prophet of the Old Covenant, and hear concerning these same mystical waters, this river of life, how well it deserves its name. 'These waters'— he too describes them as issuing from under the threshold of the temple—' go down into the desert' (a desert

---

[1] Rev. xxii. 1.

before, but by these waters changed into a Paradise, the very garden of the Lord), 'and it shall come to pass, that every thing that liveth, whithersoever the river shall come, shall live. Every thing shall live whither the river cometh.'[1] Let that river come to thee—to thy parched lips, to thy thirsty heart. Many waters thou hast drunken of hitherto, waters, it may be, of this world's best delights, and some waters, it may be feared, drawn from this world's muddiest pools. But none of them have slaked the thirst of thy soul, least of all have any of these waters which the world affords proved for thee a well of water springing up within thee unto everlasting life. Perhaps thou sayest, 'There are no such waters to slake the immortal thirst of the children of men.' But if God and his word be true, there is a river, fed from the upper springs, making glad the City of God; and every one that chooses, thou therefore if thou wilt, may take of its waters of life freely.

But, my brethren all, I must not let you go, without reminding you, as in duty bound to that Society whose cause I am pleading, of a charge which lies upon us; and I link that charge very closely with those great truths which have to-day been proclaimed in your ears. There *is* a river of life, proceeding out of the throne of God and the Lamb, which can heal all

[1] Ezek. xlvii. 1–9.

that it touches. There *is* a breath of God which can quicken and revive the dead. Oftentimes, as we look at some heathen tribe, with all its foul superstitions and wicked works, we are tempted to exclaim, 'Can these bones live?' We have received our answer. They can live; they can come together; they can stand upon their feet, armies of living men. One thing however is needful, that there should be those who should prophesy to the slain, who should bid the breath from the four winds to breathe on them that they may live. You will observe that in our vision God speaks not directly, but uses the prophet's voice, and quickens the dead through his word. It is ever so. By men God blesses men. He has constituted his Church as the instrument by which He will bless the world. Help then this Society to send forth faithful men, who shall not prophesy in vain, but at whose bidding the breath of heaven shall re-animate the slain of the earth. Show at what rate you prize your own blessings, pardon of your sins, peace with God, renewal in the spirit of your minds, the hope of heaven, by your eagerness to impart the same to others. Withhold not more than is meet. Believe the word of the wise king, who has said that such a withholding 'tendeth to poverty'[1]—to poverty of spirit, to poverty of grace, yes, and not seldom to poverty of estate too: for how

[1] Prov. xi. 24.

often, because men will not give, God takes, takes and leaves no blessing behind Him; while to them who render to Him cheerfully and freely, first themselves, for that is the condition of all acceptable offering, and then of their substance, He can and will in his own way and in his own measure cause all good things to abound.

SERMON XIX.

ALL SAINTS.

Rev. vii. 9, 10.

After this I beheld, and, lo, a great multitude, which no man could number, of all nations, and kindreds, and people, and tongues, stood before the throne, and before the Lamb, clothed with white robes, and palms in their hands; And cried with a loud voice, saying, Salvation to our God which sitteth upon the throne, and unto the Lamb.

ALL the services of to-day have helped to remind us—this sublime Scripture reminds us above all—that this is the festival of All Saints. We commemorate, that is, upon this day, not one or another pre-eminent servant of God, but all those who have lived and died in the true faith and fear of his holy name. We ask that we may be followers of them, as they were followers of Christ. We seek to derive for ourselves such help in our Christian pilgrimage as the contemplation of their lives and deaths is capable of abundantly yielding; for the language of the poet is hardly in excess, when of them he exclaims:—

> 'They are, indeed, our pillar fires,
>   Seen as we go;
> They are that City's shining spires,
>   We travel to.'

But it is not their lives and their deaths only which we are this day invited to contemplate. What a scene of glory unimaginable does the Seer of Patmos unfold before our eyes in the Scripture which you have just heard. Let us dwell on it a little. 'I beheld, and, lo, a great multitude, which no man could number.' Even so; it will have come to this—a great multitude which no man can number; and yet it is written too: 'Strait is the gate, and narrow is the way, and few there be that find it;' and again: 'Many are called, but few chosen;' and again: 'The faithful are minished from among the children of men;' and this may be, and no doubt is, true of any one age or one country; but bring them all together, of all times and of all tongues, and they will be many, a great cloud of witnesses, a vast ocean of blessedness, fed and filled as it will have been by innumerable rills.

And is not this a strengthening, elevating thought—this of that countless multitude which will one day stand before the throne? How often we are tempted to be out of all heart. The world seems so strong, and the Church seems so weak—Christianity itself almost a failure, unable to enlist the affections of men, at least of the men of this generation, impotent to contest the battle-field of the earth with the powers which are arrayed against it. Put away from you thoughts like these. They are the pleas of our indolence, the outcomings of our unbelief. The Son of God did not take our flesh, and live our life, and die our death, in vain. He has everywhere his hidden ones—in the worst times his seven thousand in Israel that have not bowed the knee to Baal [1]—precious golden grains of wheat, which shall fill the garners of heaven, and fill them even to overflowing, though they be now concealed, one here, one there, by the mountains of chaff, which shall then have been for ever winnowed away from the barn-floor of the Lord.

Is not this, I say, a cheering, sustaining thought? They may be few here or few there; but let them all be gathered into one,—all that have departed in the true faith of his holy name—from the first that fell asleep in Jesus almost as soon as He quitted the earth, or rather from righteous Abel, to him, the last that shall have hardly breathed out his latest sigh before the trump of the archangel shall recall him to that life which he had scarcely forsaken, and they will constitute this innumerable company; for indeed God would not be satisfied with less; He will have no solitudes, no empty places, no vacant thrones in heaven, but infinite

[1] Rom. xi. 4.

multitudes to be sharers in his blessedness, to declare to all creation and through all eternity the wondrous counsels of his love.

And then, dear friends, what thoughts arise in the heart as we contemplate not the numbers only, but the quarters from which all these will have been gathered —from 'all nations, and kindreds, and people, and tongues.' Those who were divided here by all which could divide, who were separated from one another by immense distances of time, of space, of culture— barbarians to one another here—yea, those who were kept asunder by far sadder barriers than these, those who misunderstood, perhaps mutually anathematised one another, until heaven would have almost seemed no heaven to them, if they had been told that they should meet each the other there, shall yet, being one in Christ, one in their faith and love to Him, stand together before the throne, and exchange the long alienations and miserable discords of earth for the blessed concords of heaven.

Think, too, from other points of view, what a marvellous company will that be! Think of all that will be there, and—awful thought!—of all that will *not* be there. Not there many who have walked in the full blaze of Gospel light; who have had all the advantages in the possession of the truth which we have; but who, knowing much, have loved not at all; whose places therefore, for there were places for them if they had shown themselves worthy of them, shall know them not; whose crowns others shall have taken; while there will be found in that wondrous company not a few who, amid much darkness, superstition, and error, have been true to the central truth of all, have clung to Jesus with full affiance of heart; and when it shall be enquired with something of wonder why this one or the other is so near to the throne, 'He loved much,' or 'She loved much,' will be the key and explanation of all. Let us not lose sight of this, for indeed it is good for us that we should always remember that while faith is the condition of salvation, there is every reason to believe that love will be the measure of blessedness.

And all these the beloved disciple saw in the visions of God standing before the throne, occupying no remote province or obscure corner of heaven, but as a kind of first-fruits of God's creatures, in whom that promise of Christ was being fulfilled, that where He was, there they should be also—He *on* the throne, and they *around* it. And he saw them 'clothed with white robes'— even as white is evermore the colour of heaven. But these white robes, white, as we may be well assured, not merely as we count whiteness, but with the dazzling whiteness of heaven, where had they gotten them? For that company, the excellent of the earth though they were, had yet travelled through a naughty world, they too gathering their spots and their stains, some deeper and darker than others; but all having gathered spots and stains out of number in this passage. How then so white now? The seer does not wait long to tell us. They had washed these robes of theirs and made them white in the blood of the Lamb.[1]

And this is not all. There are 'palms in their hands.' Now we shall lose much of the riches and beauty of this Scripture if we take, as so many interpreters have done, these palms merely as the signs and tokens of victory. Doubtless if we met words like these in some Greek or Latin poet, such an interpretation would be a just one. But the Apocalypse moves altogether in the circle of sacred imagery; all its symbols and images are derived from the Old Testament; none are borrowed from the heathen and profane world; and it is to the Old Testament that we must look for the explanation of these palms. The key of knowledge which shall unlock to us their true significance must be looked for at Lev. xxiii. 40, where Moses, instituting by divine command the Feast of Tabernacles, gives this instruction, 'And ye shall take you the boughs of goodly trees, branches of palm trees, and the boughs of thick trees, and ye shall rejoice before the Lord seven days;' and this we read at a later

[1] Ver. 14.

day of their doing: 'Therefore they bare branches, and fair boughs, and palms also, and sang praises unto him.'[1] Now keep in mind the significance of that Feast of Tabernacles, and why it was that the people were to dwell in those booths for eight days. There was here a commemoration of the weary wanderings through the desert, and of the blessed entrance into the promised land: 'that your generations may know that I made the children of Israel to dwell in booths, when I brought them out of the land of Egypt.'[2] The palms, then, are the tokens of a sorrow that has been turned into joy, of weary wanderings that have been succeeded by a blessed rest; and when these are thus placed in the hands of the redeemed, we learn by this token that they are keeping at last that true Feast of Tabernacles, whereof the other was but the feeble antitype, that their pilgrimage through the great and terrible wilderness of the world is for ever ended; and that now 'they shall hunger no more, neither thirst any more; neither shall the sun light on them, nor any heat.'

Will not that be much? Will not that be a blessed consummation? When we call to mind what a forlorn and desert journey for multitudes of God's saints this earthly life has been, or now is; all the bitterness which they have known to themselves, and with which no stranger has intermeddled; the unappeased hunger

---

[1] Macc. x. 7.   [2] Lev. xxiii. 43.

of so many souls after a love which they here have never found; when we picture to ourselves all the youthful brows from which the fresh garlands, a springing hope and joy, have been early and for ever stricken; when we think of the tragedy to which multitudes of lives, showing so fairly at the outset, have presently turned; of the great tribulation through which so many pass to their rest, the fire-chariots of pain by which God's saints are so often rapt into his presence; when we contemplate a little the marvel and the mystery of all that unutterable anguish which He often suffers here to be the portion of his beloved, is it not well to be reminded that however this may endure for the night, yet joy cometh in the morning; that there are festal palms for the weariest pilgrim of this world, and an innumerable multitude of happy palmers standing before the throne? And some of these perhaps we have known; some of them, it may be, were once bound up here in the same bundle of life with ourselves; and these so beautiful in their lives, so beautiful in their deaths, that only to remember that such have been, that we have walked for a season with them, is a chastening, a purifying, yea, and however much we may miss and mourn them, a gladdening thought. And we who are struggling and contending still, shall we not, on this day above all, praise our God for them: that He is holding them in safest keeping, in the hollow of his hand, in the repose of his Paradise, in the secret of his pavilion? Shall we not find in the very remembrance of them, a remembrance which is a communion as well, a new motive to holiness, lest in the end there should be set a great gulf between ourselves and them?

Oh that to us it may be granted to have a place with them, were it only in the outermost circle of those concentric rings of light and life and glory, which, each one nearer than the other, surround the throne, and draw joy unutterable from the beatific vision of Him who sits upon the throne! And there is but one way for this, and that way the Gospel of this morning, the eight Beatitudes of the Sermon upon the Mount, has taught us—brought as that portion of Scripture is in our Prayer Book into wonderful juxtaposition with *this*. It is the poor in spirit, the mourning, the meek, the hungering and thirsting after righteousness, the merciful, the pure in heart, the peacemakers, the persecuted for righteousness' sake; it is these, and only these, who make up that great multitude which stand before the throne, and before the Lamb.

SERMON XX.

THE HOLY WOMEN AT THE CROSS.

JOHN xix. 25.

Now there stood by the cross of Jesus his mother, and his mother's sister, Mary the wife of Cleophas, and Mary Magdalene.

THEY understood not the meaning, certainly not all the meaning, of that spectacle which was before them, that weeping company who on that world-memorable day stood by the Cross of Jesus—neither she, the mother, who now at length found the word of the aged Simeon true—'yea, a sword shall pierce through thine own soul also'—nor that other Mary, the greatly sinning, and the greatly loving and greatly forgiven. No, nor yet the Apostle who testified of these things, and who, as we gather from the verse which follows my text, having recovered from his brief fear, was also standing there, that he might receive the last legacy of love at the hands of his dying Lord. They understood it not all—as yet the mighty mystery of that atoning sacrifice had only obscurely revealed itself to their eyes; they saw but darkly through the thick cloud of a present agony how that Cross was indeed an altar, *the* altar, the true altar, to which every other altar that had been ever reared pointed—from which alone they derived any meaning at all.

And when all this became plain to them, as presently it did become plain, what new and further mysteries must they presently have found in that Cross —what an even deeper significance must that which they had witnessed have acquired in their eyes. And how indeed should it have been otherwise? For the things of Christ, and especially the things of the Cross of Christ, are things which angels desire to look into, which angels themselves do not hope to fathom.

And yet, while all this is so, while the mystery of that Cross is unsearchable, while we can never know all that it meant, yet at the same time there is much that we *can* know. If it has hidden things which only eternity can make clear, it has also most plain things for the present time. Indeed there never was before, there can never be again, so plain a speaking to the world. That Cross has a voice clearer than every other voice; it speaks a language more impossible to be mistaken. Let us only in spirit be gathered near it, let us only be found in company with the faithful ones that are there, with the holy mother blessed and now afflicted above women, with the Magdalen and with John, and there will come out to us voices from that

Cross, which will speak to us in deeper depths of our being than any other voices that have ever reached us from elsewhere. All that is needed on our part is earnestly to ask that we may learn the lesson which it is set to teach us; that we may read the meaning of our lives, and the meaning of the world around us, in the light which is shed upon them from it.

And first, brethren, how shall we dare with that Cross in our view, with that Cross lifted up before us, to lay out our lives for self-pleasing and self-indulging? I am not speaking here of those grosser forms of self-indulgence, which are evidently and plainly sinful, and still less of open and manifest sins, which go before men to judgment, which they who do declare plainly that they have no part nor lot with Him who came to deliver men from their unrighteousness and their sins. But how shall we venture to lay out our lives for ourselves—how shall we make the possessing of this world's honours, or its wealth, or its favour, or its high places, the main end and scope of our lives? how shall we dare with that thorn crown in view and all the concentrated agony of that hour, to live lives, as far as we can make them so, of unbroken luxury and ease, taking no part in the sufferings of Christ which we can avoid, choosing ever the feast and never the fast; choosing to sleep with them that slept in the garden, rather than to pray with Him, who being in an agony, prayed the more earnestly; so that when a Lent is passed and all its blessed assistances for setting forward our soul's health have escaped us unimproved, our Lord's words of a mournful reproach, 'What, could ye not watch one hour?' or the sadder and more reproachful yet, 'Sleep on now,' sound only too mournfully and appropriately in our ears.

I say, brethren, with Christ's Cross before us, shall we attempt to shrink from and evade our own? In truth, a hopeless endeavour! for he who will not *take* his share in the world's burden, who draws his shoulder from under it, does not really escape it. His share of that burden is laid upon him still. All that he has effected by his attempt to shun, is that he misses the blessing of it. He has sought to save his life, and so perhaps has lost it. For thus it is ever. 'Care finds the careless out.' In a moment it leaps within the defences which a man may ever so carefully have reared; in a moment the enemy is within those defences; and all the thought and labour of a life to exclude him has proved vain: and he whose labour it was that he might not have a crumpled rose-leaf under him, finds himself tossing suddenly upon a bed of thorns: he, who would not touch with his little finger his brethren's burdens, now groans under his own. For even so does a righteous God evermore defeat men's plans of self-pleasing, and Himself lays upon them that, and often in far larger measure, which they would not *take* upon themselves. We have but this choice, to meet the toil and the task of life as manful combatants, or to be overtaken by them as cowardly fugitives. In one way or other these will inevitably be ours.

Therefore for these, and for all other reasons, looking at the Cross of Christ, let us dare to say to ourselves, In the power of that Cross I will die to myself, to my own will, to my own desires, in so far as they are mine, and not God's. It is an awful word, when we say it in earnest—when we say it, really meaning to carry it out—really meaning that it shall be the death-knell of our own self-will and self-pleasing which has sounded, and all in us of the old man will plead and remonstrate against it, will urge that life is not worth living on such conditions as these. Yet if thou dare to say it and to act upon it, thou shalt find that out of this death of the old man, shall presently come life, even the true life which was utterly cramped and confined before — this seeming bondage shall be thy truest liberty; this which seems utter straitness for thy spirit, shall anon translate thy feet into a large room. At the same time let us not suppose, dear friends, that it will be enough to say once that we will die to self, and that this once resolutely said, the struggle will be over, the victory will have been gained. We shall need to say it again and again; for on every side we shall find the love of luxury, of ease, of pleasure, in short, of the world, encroaching upon us, which ever and again will need to be arrested and thrust back. Hardly, and only with earnest prayer and after many a struggle, do we win a foot of ground here, and still more hardly do we keep that we have won. To stamp the Cross upon our lives and on all parts of them, this is no slight undertaking. What continual danger we are in, of slipping out of this, of finding some excuse for not attempting this. How ready is each one of us to smooth away all the rough corners and sharp edges of Christian obedience, all which brings us in unwelcome collision with the world, or with our own desires— or to let the world by its constant yet almost imperceptible friction smooth away for us these rough corners and edges. And yet if that Cross means anything (if Christ hanging there was in any sense a pattern and example to us), all this in the power of his Spirit must be attempted, and in a measure must be done. Here then is our first lesson. That Cross witnesses against lives which, stained it may be with no great sins, are yet marked by no great self-devotion; which, perhaps without excess, are yet also without self-denial—lives which in the world's sight and world's estimate are decent and comely, and would have indeed been so, if no Saviour had suffered, and in suffering shown us a more excellent way, and commanded us to walk in it.

But secondly, in what light does that Cross show to us a life, not such as I have spoken of, of ordinary decent worldliness, but of positive sin and open transgression of the divine law—that Cross of Christ, upon which He condemned sin in the flesh? Oh, brethren, it is just this Cross which throws so fearful a light upon sin now, which will make it in the world to come so impossible to be forgiven. It will be the thorn-crowned brow, whose gaze it will be so dreadful hereafter to meet. On his head who shall be our Judge, there will be many crowns, but the crown of thorns, as it is the most glorious, so will it be the most awful of all. It will be the nailed and the pierced hand which it will be so crushing to have laid on us in anger. It will be his cup of gall, which will have made our cup of sinful pleasure so guilty a thing. To have resisted the mighty attractions of the Cross, this will be the great condemnation of sinners—to have made, as far as in them lay, that word of the Saviour vain, 'I, if I be lifted up, will draw all men unto me.' It had been comparatively little to have stood out against the threatenings of righteousness; but that when God Himself laid bare to us his beating heart, and bade us to cast ourselves there, his wounded side that we might hide ourselves in it, then to have sullenly stood aloof, to have gone upon our own ways, and to have stopped our ears and made them adder deaf to the mighty charmings of love, this will be the sin of sin, the sin which will defy forgiveness.

SERMON XXI.

CHRIST POOR THAT WE MIGHT BE RICH.

2 COR. viii. 9.

Ye know the grace of our Lord Jesus Christ, that, though he was rich, yet for your sakes he became poor, that ye through his poverty might be rich.

IT was but recently that these Corinthians had known this grace of the Lord Jesus Christ, for it was he himself, the writer of these words, who had first brought to them the knowledge of that grace; who had found them, some the servants of vain idols, and some of a vain philosophy—or some, it might be, the servants of both at the same time—and, delivering them from these sinful and beggarly elements of this world, had imparted to them the knowledge of those unsearchable riches of Christ, whereof he here reminds them. And if you will observe the occasion *on* which, and the motive *with* which he utters these words, you will find them to be as follows: The Church at Corinth was comparatively a wealthy one—above all, wealthy if set beside the mother Church at Jerusalem. From some cause or another, various causes have been assigned, the poor saints at Jerusalem continually needed the assistance of their richer brethren throughout the world; and St. Paul is here urging the Christians at Corinth to a liberal contribution on their behalf. And now the apostle, who loves ever to appeal to the highest motives, sets before the Corinthians, in these words of my text, why it was their duty to open their hands and their hearts freely, to respond cheerfully and largely to the appeal which he made to them. Ye profess to be followers of the Lord Jesus Christ, to be desirous to walk in his footsteps, to take Him for a pattern and example. And you know what that pattern and example was—what his grace towards us was—rich He became poor for our sakes, that we, through his poverty, might be rich. Shall we refuse to follow, though it be at an infinite distance, in his footsteps? How infinite this distance is, and must always continue, and at the same time how constraining the motive which we may here find for acts of self-sacrifice and self-denial, be they small or be they great, will appear most plainly, when we have a little more closely studied the memorable words: 'Ye know the grace of our Lord Jesus Christ, who being rich, he, etc.' *Being rich,* or *though He was rich;* to what do these words refer? What were the riches which He had, and which for our sakes He renounced? No doubt the riches of his glory and pre-eminence in heaven—in his præ-existent subsistence—

the glory which He had with the Father, before the foundations of the world were laid. All attempts to explain away these words, as though they expressed less than this, as though anything short of this would exhaust and satisfy their meaning, must at once be rejected and set aside as idle and futile. He was *rich*—what words of ours can express, for indeed what thoughts of ours can conceive, the riches which were his? He was in the form of God, the firstborn or the born before every creature—in the bosom of the Father—sharing with the Father and the Holy Ghost the incommunicable bliss of Deity, for He thought it not robbery to be equal with God, and taking all, did not account that He was snatching anything which was not rightfully his own. And Him the angels, a living circle of light around the throne, worshipped for evermore; and when the four living creatures gave glory and honour and thanks to Him that sat upon the throne, who liveth for ever and ever, it was to Him, to the Son, the Image of the Invisible God, that this glory and honour and these thanks were rendered.

But being rich He made himself poor. Here again what comparison drawn from things earthly would make even a remote approximation to this making of Himself poor on the part of the Son of God? Truly it immeasurably transcends them all. It is a real fall when a king, by the turn of fortune's wheel, comes down to a private man's estate; but we have a far greater fall than this to deal with. Let him exchange his royal robes for a beggar's weeds, his sceptre for a staff, wander an outcast and an exile over the earth, that too were nothing—that would but feebly help to shew forth what we are contemplating here.

For such a change, great as no doubt it would be, would yet find place altogether within fixed and in some respects very narrow limits—that is, within the limits and conditions of our humanity. That king who left his throne—he was but a man at the highest, subject therefore to all the infirmities of our nature, to sorrow, to sickness, to accidents, to death, dwelling in a house of clay which the moth crushes—he continues a man at his lowest. He has but changed his outward garb and trappings, not the essentials of his existence.

A rich man to become a poor man, or a great man a small, or a king a beggar—what is it after all, wherein does it even remotely approach the change which St. Paul speaks of here: God to become man, not to cease from being God, for that it was impossible for Him to do. God could never cease to be God; but to abdicate and renounce for the time all the actings of Deity, to empty Himself of all these, to take upon Him man's nature with all its inherent weaknesses and infirmities, with all the conditions which cling to it, except, indeed, its sin—which is only its miserable accidents and not its essence—to take upon Him the form of a servant, and as lowest and last and least to walk this painful earth of ours, hungering and thirsting, having not where to lay his head, enduring the contradictions of sinners, and at length paying the things which He never took, stripped of all, bare of all, undergoing the extreme penalty of our sin, tasting death and the bitterness of death for every man. Truly He made Himself poor for our sakes—a worm and no man. There was no poverty like his.

But his purpose in all this. *That we through his poverty should be rich.* How strangely these words sound! that the poverty of one should be the riches of many! And yet it is indeed only another putting of the same wonderful paradox which runs through the whole Gospel, and through the whole of Christ's dealings with the children of men. Those dealings were throughout a giving and a taking, a wondrous exchange, such as it could only have entered into the heart of God to conceive. He everywhere taking from us whatever was poorest, meanest, saddest, most painful, most ignominious, and giving to us what was highest, noblest, choicest, best, and most glorious; taking earth and giving heaven, taking our poverty and giving to us his riches. But this is not all; taking our shame and giving to us his glory, taking our cross and giving to us his crown, taking our sin and giving to us his righteousness, taking our curse and giving to us his blessing, taking our death and giving to us his life.

Truly He did make Himself poor that we through his poverty might be rich. But of what riches speaks the Apostle here? Not of silver and gold, corruptible things, of which if one have more another must have less, which oftentimes corrupt those that have them, which at best perish in the using; which leave us, or which at the best we must leave. Not to make us rich in these; for He knew that man's true life was not in them, that a man abounding in these, rich in all which the world calls riches, might yet still be poor, poor in all the elements of true happiness, poor in time and poor for eternity; poor in time, having no joy in his life here, for the fountains of joy even here are within a man and not without, from above and not from beneath. How poor too may a rich man of this world be, how poor for eternity, how bare, how naked, how miserable, when that world which was his only world shall have passed away from him and the glory of it; this too He knew as none of us *can* know, as it is to be hoped we shall never know, as only that last and terrible day shall declare.

To make us rich, then, in what? Rich in peace, rich in joy, rich in the grace, favour, presence, and benediction of our God. And oh! brethren, how poor is man's life, how mean, how wretched, if it have not these; if it be lived without Christ and without God. Men may array that life outwardly with what gorgeous trappings they can; cover over and conceal the inner squalor and meanness of it as they will; they may hide its loathsome sores under purple and gold; yet the inner meanness and poverty of it cannot effectually be hid, will make themselves felt; its sores refuse to be hidden, will break forth so that all may see them. There is hollowness at the heart of a worldly life, be it outwardly as rich and prosperous as it may; a want of sincerity in its joys; its mirth is madness, and its loudest laughter ever followed by a sigh. What good shall my life do me? is sooner or later the cry of the jaded votary of pleasure. He who thought to enjoy everything in a little while enjoys nothing. The prodigal of yesterday is the bankrupt of to-day. 'I enjoy nothing,' those were the very words of one, gifted with all the external helps to happiness—a poet, one of the noble of the earth, gifted with genius, with all that wealth could command, who, having loosed himself from all the painful tasks which duty would impose, sought only to please himself. Having laid himself out to enjoy everything, but without God, against God, this was the sad and forlorn confession which was wrung from his lips ere he had reached half the allotted years of man.

But that Saviour with whom we have to do makes the life of his people rich, brings them back to God, the one fountain and spring of all joy, reconciles them to Him in the blood of his cross, and in that same act reconciles them to themselves, healing the deep hurt of their spirits and changing the deep discords of their lives into harmonies. The world in which they live, they behold it now as God's world. The work appointed to them to do is God's work, and this adds dignity and honour to the humblest task which may be allotted to them here.

Toil and labour, sorrow and suffering, all have transformed and transfigured from the moment that the light of heaven, the light of Christ's cross has rested upon them. They are no longer mere heavy crushing burdens, under which our suffering humanity groans as it staggers wearily to its grave; but these very things, seeming to be burdens, are indeed lightsome wings, lifting us heavenward; a divine training and discipline appointed for the children of God; a ladder let down from heaven, by which they may mount, painfully, it may be, and with bleeding feet to the throne of God. Surely the Apostle had good right to affirm that Jesus Christ became poor that we through his poverty might be rich.

But whom did St. Paul mean by *we*? Was it only those who were already partakers of these riches that were in Christ; and who should henceforward glorify themselves in the exclusive possession of these riches?

or was it not rather all men—that all whom sin had impoverished might through the grace of our Lord Jesus Christ be made rich? It was not a favoured few, but all whose poverty Christ would fain change into riches, their sin into righteousness, their shame into glory, their despair into hope, their death in life into a life even in death; his purposes of love as wide as the world.

SERMON XXII.

LOT'S CHOICE.

GEN. xiii. 12, 13.

Abram dwelled in the land of Canaan, and Lot dwelled in the cities of the plain, and pitched his tent toward Sodom. But the men of Sodom were wicked and sinners before the Lord exceedingly.

Lot, I need not remind you, was a nephew of Abraham, his brother's son; and when Abraham at the bidding of God made his great venture of faith, quitted his father's house and father's gods, and began his long pilgrimage in the land of promise, he took, we are told, Lot as the companion of his pilgrimage. You will observe the entirely subordinate position as is slightly but sufficiently indicated by the words of the sacred historian: Abraham took Lot—no slight or trivial honour to be thus brought into closest fellowship with such a man as Abraham, one of the noblest that ever trod this earth of ours, the friend of God; in some sort the founder of the glorious family of the children of God, for indeed to live in near familiarity with one nobler than ourselves, with higher ideals of life, is a talent for which we shall have to give an account. How far Lot was ennobled by such companionship with one of the born kings of the earth, what spiritual uses he made of such an opportunity, we shall presently see. The first occasion on which there was room for a display on his part was that of the strife which sprang up between the herdsmen of the greater and the lesser man. Both had numerous herds of cattle till the land was not large enough to find room for both. They must part. And now each shows himself in his true light; money, goods of this present world, dividing of the inheritance, these and such like do more perhaps than aught else in the world to lay bare what men really are, touchstones to distinguish truly between the false and the true. So it proved here. Abraham the royal hearted bears himself nobly, he is the uncle, Lot but the nephew, he already the recipient of the glorious promises of God, in whom all the kindreds of the earth should be blest. Lot the nephew, one who in his insignificance would never have been so much as heard of in after years.

But Abraham claims nothing for himself on the score of all this; gives his nephew the pick and choice of the whole land which is before him. If thou wilt take the right hand, then I will take the left. And Lot is content to profit by the offer of his uncle. Without remonstrance, without real reluctance, without so much as the show and semblance of reluctance, he at once selects for himself what appears the best. Then 'Lot lifted up his eyes, and beheld all the plain of Jordan, that it was well watered every where, then Lot chose him all the plain of Jordan,' not a share or portion of what was best, but all of it for himself, and pitched his tent toward Sodom. Surely, if there had been any true greatness in him, it would have been impossible for him to have availed himself in this fashion of the large-heartedness of Abraham and without more ado have appropriated all which seemed best to himself. Even in selfishness, even among the children of this world, in greedy graspings there are measures, proportions, and degrees.

But there were other moral blemishes which cleaved to the choice which Lot had made, only too suggestive of what was the true spirit of the man about whom we are now concerned. The sacred historian, having recorded that Lot pitched his tent towards Sodom, adds these significant words: 'but the men of Sodom were wicked and sinners before the Lord exceedingly.' Observe here how the sacred historian leaves us to put these two things together to form our own judgment of him who for such poor and paltry gains was willing to plant himself, his wife, his children in the midst of a people so deeply sunken in impure lusts, and yet wherefore should we wonder at the silence of our God, and if there are many things which we must read *into* Scripture, there are also many which we must read *out* of it. The silences of Scripture are also as instructive as its speech; what it does *not* say will often convey lessons as real, as effective, as what it does say. Thus we are not told in as many words how miserable a falling away it was for a member of the elect family to mingle with the heathen and to learn their works. We are left to gather all this from the after issues of the story. Lot's life is a sermon, it was meant to be a sermon to himself, let it in any event be a sermon for us. Lot makes haste to be rich, but the riches escape him. The good which he had chosen is no good, the people of Sodom with whom he has cast his lot, were defeated in battle, the city in which he has chosen to live is taken, Lot and all that he has is swept away in what would have been hopeless captivity if Abraham had not played the man indeed, pursued the enemies who were retiring, laden with their spoils, overtaken them with his little company of faithful retainers, and rescued his nephew and all from the terrible doom that was his.

One would have thought that this was enough, that Lot would have shaken off the dust of the guilty city; that, however fair, however well watered the plain of Sodom might be, he would not have put himself in the way of being again partaker of her plagues. But there are some on whom all the dealings of God are thrown away, whom his gentleness does not make great, whose severity does not warn. And Lot was one of these. When we next hear of him, we find him comfortably established at Sodom again, sitting at the door of his house, improved and repaired as I do not doubt, and all this as zealously as though nothing had happened, as though nothing would happen; as though there were no such things as warnings in the world, and where these are neglected and despised, judgments that follow behind them. That fierce tempest of war in which all was so nearly perishing together for him and his has past over.

All shows fair and prosperous again, though indeed a judgment far more terrible than that which they had just overlived was at hand, even at the door. As concerns the sinful cities, the cup of their iniquity was full, they were just about to be set forth, suffering the vengeance of eternal fire. Neither can Lot do anything to avert this doom. There are righteous men whose prayers can save a soul, a city, a kingdom, that is, if there be anything savable about them. There are righteous men whose mere presence imposes a restraint upon the wicked, so that these, whether they will or not, stand in awe and abashed before goodness which rises to such immeasurable heights above them. But Lot was evidently not one of these, when he protests against and would fain prevent a hideous crime, all the reply which he gets from those among whom he has been living is this: 'This one fellow came in to sojourn, and he will needs be a judge.' Nobody, it is evident, makes much account of him or of anything which he says or does. When having been warned of the approaching overthrow of the city, the winding sheet of fire in which it was about to be wrapped, he goes to his sons-in-law with words like these: 'Get you out of this place, for the Lord will destroy this city,' his words carry no weight, obtain no belief from them. He seemed to his sons-in-law as one that mocked. Nay, his wife herself, who must have known him best, does not believe him, but looking back in the very agony of her flight courts the dreadful doom which overtook her. Indeed, one may affirm, that he himself hardly credited the message he brought to others; we are expressly told that he lingered, could hardly be torn away from the precious things of earth to which his soul so clung, was only delivered from perishing with the perishing city by the gracious violence of an angel, which saved him as in his own despite. But it is life, and life only, which he has saved; all else is gone, all which he has gotten by preferring himself in honour and profit to others on that memorable day when they two, uncle and nephew, separated and went their several ways to issues so different; all which he has gotten by taking up his abode with the wicked, that is gone too. It is not much that we hear of him more; and certainly nothing that alters for the better our estimate of his character. A little more we are told about him, but that may be passed over here. And then, with the brand of dishonour on his brow, he disappears from sacred story.

My brethren, is a life in its moral features at all resembling this the life which we should wish to have lived? To him who lived that life, who lived a life set at so low a key, there were not wanting, even in that poor spiritual condition, many tokens of the faithfulness of God—for indeed what faithfulness it is in Him when He deals with us as He dealt with Lot in blended judgment and mercy—when He empties us from vessel to vessel, when He breaks our idols, defeats our schemes of wealth, disappoints our ambitions, strips us, it may be, of everything which we clung to the most—when, I say, He does this instead of leaving us to wrap ourselves in the robe of an unhallowed prosperity, with no sorrows in our life, and no bonds in our death, with all things going well with us except the one thing which in the end will be all.

But, my brethren, this faithfulness of our God which will not leave us alone in our sins, which will not leave us to the saddest and dreadfullest of all dooms, namely, the unpunished prosperity of wicked, or say worldly men, we cannot say that it always accomplishes its work. I had almost said that it failed in *his* case with whom we have mainly now to do—but, leaving this in the obscurity in which Scripture has left it, this certainly we may affirm that, if saved, Lot was saved as by fire. Would we wish such a *scarcely saved* as this to be ours, graces so poor and so stunted as his were, little service or none done by us to others, little or no glory done by us to God—and then, after many warnings which yet had failed to warn us, a close to our day of grace with as little of honour about it as waited on the close of this man's day; no abundant entrance into the kingdom ours, but we cast naked and shivering, as shipwrecked mariners, on the shores of everlasting life?

Assuredly we would not have it so—and blessed be God, He can appoint for us quite another course for our Christian life, and quite other issues for it, issues happy and honourable, if only, in quite another sense than Lot's, we will choose the better part for ourselves; if only we seek to be gilded with touches, however faint, of brightness, such as are to be gotten by habitual fellowship with the excellent of the earth; above all, by communion with Him who is fairer than the children of men, and who makes fair, in a manner transfiguring and transforming all who steadfastly look at Him and behold, in however slight a measure, his glory—all this,

I say, may be ours, if, laying God's judgments to heart, we turn our backs betimes on the doomed and guilty city of this world, we blessed fugitives to that heavenly city which hath foundation, a city of refuge now, and of glory for evermore.

SERMON XXIII.

THE STUDY OF SCRIPTURE.

Rom. xv. 4.

Whatsoever things were written aforetime were written for our learning, that we through patience and comfort of the scriptures might have hope.

It is much to be feared that the acquaintance which too many among us possess with those many sacred books which together constitute for us the Bible is very slight and very superficial, that it is sadly wanting in thoroughness, accuracy, extent, and depth. There are certain portions of Scripture with which almost all of us can scarcely help having more or less familiarity— the Gospels for example, and those chapters in the Old Testament which we have heard from year to year read in the Sunday service of the Church. But for too many among us there is just reason to suspect all beyond this is, I will not say an unknown, a *terra incognita*, but one which has been very carelessly explored, if indeed explored at all. The hold which they have on the great facts, features, and outlines of the rest of the Bible is of the loosest and slightest kind, while even those who possess a livelier interest in spiritual things could only too easily be carried beyond the lines to which their knowledge extends. Familiar, it may be, with the highways of Scripture, they are yet comparative strangers to its byways—have rarely or never trodden these, though much, if not as much, of profit and instruction is to be gathered in these which I have ventured to call its byways, as in its more frequented highways.

What is the explanation of this prevailing unacquaintance with Scripture, this lack of a close familiarity which I fear we must charge home upon so many, not merely with its lesser details, but with its broader features and outlines? The explanation, alas! is only too easy. The Bible is little read, and is studied still less. We rejoice as members of a Reformed Church in an open Bible, that no tyrannous priesthood keeps the Word of God under lock and key, dispensing just such little petty doles and portions of it as it pleases to the lay people. We glory in our societies which circulate copies of the Scriptures by thousands and by millions; that it is not now as in those ages before the invention of printing, when a copy of the Bible would cost some forty pounds of our present money, while it now costs fewer pence; but ah! brethren, what profits an open Bible, a Bible so cheap that it has been or may be brought into nearly every cottage of the land, if at the same time it remains an unread Bible? What profits the commonness of the blessing if this very commonness has taken away in great part from the price and value of it? What is our gain if it should appear that the Word of the Lord was precious in those days, and is not precious in ours?

Brethren, I appeal to the consciences of some among us, and they shall answer whether I express too unfavourable a judgment of our present religious condition, when I affirm that at this day the Bible is very little read among us—little read, I mean, as compared to the claims which it has upon every one among us. There is one person with whose ways, doings, habits, thoughts, duties, manner of distributing his time, each of us here present is thoroughly acquainted. How is it with that one person—namely, with ourselves? I speak not here of those who are altogether negligent of this duty, such as in habit and practice never *read* the Bible. They may perhaps take it down from its shelf in an hour of sickness or pain, to be quickly replaced there so soon as that sickness has been exchanged for health and the pain for ease; or, it may be, in the season of great sorrow and bereavement they turn to its unfamiliar pages, hoping to find some comfort there; but the stress of the sorrow passes away, and the volume is gladly closed and set aside in some unknown corner again. But there are others who, though they would not admit this entire neglect of the Word of God, must yet own that their only reading of the Bible is on Sunday. A chapter, or a chapter or two, read on the Sunday evening is all the searching of the Scriptures for which they fancy they can find time—is, at any rate, all for which they have heart or desire.

And you, dear friends, who are more habitual students of God's Word, who daily seek to nourish your souls with some portions of it, must not you, or at least some of you, acknowledge that these portions are often small, the amount of time allotted to this study only too brief, often encroached on from divers sides, so that while the Scripture may be read indeed, yet it is not also marked, learned, and inwardly digested, and that thus the profit is small as compared to what it should have been. There is not on your part all that growing familiarity and increasing acquaintance with the oracles of God which there should be.

For, indeed, brethren, there is no book which requires such constant, such daily study, if we are to become familiar with it, if we are at all to make the riches which it contains our own. Regard it first merely on what one might call its *human* side, and quite apart from the fact that it is the wisdom not of man but of God. Consider first the mere size of the book. The Bible contains some twelve hundred chapters. Is it a light matter to become familiar with a volume of such extent as this? And then consider the infinite variety of the matter which it contains: books so unlike one another—books of history, books of poetry, books of prophecy, books of doctrine. Consider also, that while there is in this book the highest method (for method is of God), there is no system in it (for systems are of men). Scripture is not a *hortus siccus*, where you can at once find each thing which you want to find, labelled and ticketed, and put away in its own drawer; it is not a *hortus siccus*, with everything under your hand at once, but a garden; and that not an artificial garden, in which can be everywhere traced the hand and art and device of man, but a glorious wilderness of sweets, in which under higher guidance—guidance of the Spirit of God, guidance of the Church of God—you must gradually learn to find your way, and discover one by one the beauties which it contains, but which it is very far from obtruding upon every careless observer. Assume for an instant that Scripture differs in no essential thing from the highest works of human intellect and genius—and then, as other books demand patience and study before they give up their secrets, can it be expected that this book, or rather this multitude of books, should not demand the same?

But regard the Scriptures in its proper dignity,

with those higher claims which it has upon us, as the message of God to sinful man, and then it will be still more manifest that only the constant and diligent student can hope to possess himself of any considerable portion of the treasures which it contains. For what, indeed, is Scripture? Men uttered it, but men who were moved thereto by the Holy Ghost. It is the wisdom of God. Think you that the plummet line of man, even of man enlightened by a light from on high, can soon sound the depths of the wisdom of God? Are not the depths of that wisdom unsearchable, such as we should always search *into*, but which we can never hope to search *out*. If all Scripture is by inspiration of God, and all Scripture profitable for instruction in righteousness, must not all Scripture, putting aside a very few chapters indeed, be the object of our most diligent heed?

True it is that, with all our studies, we shall never have mastered, or nearly mastered it all. We may see an end of all other perfection; but of the perfection of God, or of ought which bears a direct impress and stamp of God, we cannot see an end. Did we live a thousand years, and were we to devote the most patient industry and the rarest gifts of intellect during all this time to the study of God's Word, there would still remain in it heights which we had not scaled, depths which we had not fathomed. We should feel at the last something as Sir Isaac Newton felt when, contemplating the discoveries in natural science which he had made, and the much which remained undiscovered still at the end of his life, he exclaimed, he had been but as a child gathering up a few shells upon the shore of an illimitable ocean.

But because Scripture cannot all be known, this is no reason why we should not seek to know of it all that we can; and if there are in it veins of precious ore, which lie so far below the surface that no skill of ours can ever penetrate there, remember that there are *on* the surface waving harvests of golden grain—these within the reach of all; there is no reaper who goes forth into the fields of Scripture, but may presently return rejoicing, and bring his sheaves with him. Or look at it under another image, and it is the tree of life, planted by the waters of life, whose leaves are for medicine, and whose fruit for food—and bearing its twelve manner of fruit. Some of this fruit may grow on the topmost branches, beyond our reach; but the lowest in stature among us may gather enough to satisfy the hunger of his soul, to nourish it up unto everlasting life.

I beseech you, brethren, esteem at its due rate this inestimable gift of God to the world, even his own

Word, only inferior in value to the gift of his dear Son—and the necessary complement of that other gift—for how without a written Scripture should we have had any faithful and authentic record of the words and works of Christ? Suppose these had been entrusted to oral tradition, had been so handed down from generation to generation, how little confidence should we have that we now possessed the very words which Christ spake, a record of his works exactly as He wrought them—nay, how certain it is that we should *not* possess this, that many fables would by this time have mingled with the truth, and that it would be often impossible to distinguish one from the other. Without a Bible, the work of redemption which Christ wrought could only have reached after ages as a dim uncertain rumour, a tradition in which the elements of truth and falsehood would long before this time have been so inextricably mingled together that it would be impossible to separate them the one from the other. The one gift of a Saviour drew after it, and made necessary, a Scripture to testify of that Saviour; and a Church to be the guardian of that Scripture.

Review, I beseech you brethren every one, the relation in which you stand to the Word of God. The Church, by her collect which I have just used, specially invites you to this. If you have hitherto been content with such desultory acquaintance with it as you might pick up at church, or as you derived from the not wholly effaced recollections of childish years, resolve that this shall be so no more; that you will not wrong your soul as you have done, stinting or depriving it altogether of its necessary food.

Resolve, then, I would say first, that every day you will read some portion of Scripture, consider which the Church suggests; find, or if you cannot find, make a time for this. At any cost, at any sacrifice, rescue and redeem the time necessary for this. Remember what the Psalmist could say: 'Mine eyes prevent the night watches, that I might meditate in thy word.' Might it not sometimes so fare with you? And what you read, strive to read it devoutly—with reverence; here, too, in the spirit of the Psalmist when he exclaimed, 'Open thou mine eyes, that I may behold wondrous things out of thy law.' Remember that it is only in God's light that we can see light—that we can only see in Scripture what He shows us. The fountain from which Hagar should have quenched her thirst was close to her, and yet she could not see it. She, with her child, would have perished for thirst in the wilderness, if the angel of God had not opened her eyes, and shewed to her the fountain there (Gen. xxi. 16, 19). Christ, and Christ only, has the key of knowledge—that when He opens none can shut; that if He should shut them against our presumption and pride, not all the wise, nor all the wisdom of this world could open them to us.

Then once more let us read, looking for Christ—Christ in the Old Testament quite as much as in the New—though Christ under types and shadows in the one, and openly declared in the other. He said Himself of us: 'They testify of me, that is their glory.'

Then, too, let us read with personal application; for Scripture is like a good portrait, which, wherever we move, appears to have its eyes on us still; and many times the sacred archer may seem to have drawn his bow at a venture, but has arrows which shall pierce and penetrate through the rifts of our armour, putting us to wholesome pain, and wounding, but only wounding that they might heal.

Finally, brethren, whatever we learn out of God's Holy Word, let us seek in our lives to fulfil the same—not forgetful hearers or readers, not like a man beholding his natural face in a glass, and going his way, and straightway forgetting what manner of man he was. If that faithful mirror shews us blemishes and deformities on the face of our soul, let us seek to remove them; evil passions and tempers allowed, let us seek of God's grace to subdue them; duties undone, let us seek henceforth to fulfil them, ever striving to bring both the outward course and inward spirit of our lives into closer and more perfect agreement with what there we read.

In all these ways let us give diligence to bring out for ourselves the riches and glory of the Word of God; and then, if some gainsayer should rise up in our time —and such in all times there will be, for the Scripture, like the Scripture's Lord, shall be a sign spoken against —the objections and cavils of such objector will trouble us very little. We may not be able to answer them; it may need more learning, more ability, than we possess, but we shall have this answer: 'I *know* that Scripture is a book of God's, for I have found it so. It has answered my deepest needs. It has told me things about myself, things about God, which I could have never discovered of myself, but which, being discovered, I must at once set my seal to, as true communion with this book makes me wiser, better, purer, exerts an influence upon me for good immeasurably higher than that which is exercised by any other book—other books exercising the same only in the measure that they share the spirit of this Book. The Bible is thus to me its own attestation; I see it in its own light.' Be able to say this, let it have thus commended itself to your conscience, and your faith in Scripture, as the very Word of God, will not be shaken by any captious cavils of men; and then, though the cry be raised by some: 'What is this book more than another?' you will be able to reply that in this it is more than any other; that it exercises an influence, purifying, ennobling, strengthening, on the hearts and lives of those who study it and love it, which no other book can lay claim to in the least; and that you yourselves have found this so.

SERMON XXIV.

BAXTER AND 'THE SAINT'S REST.'

HEBREWS iv. 9.

There remaineth therefore a rest to the people of God.

I HAVE undertaken to speak to you this day of one, and of the most famous work of one, who at the time of his death stood outside of, and to a certain point in antagonism to, that Church, whereof most, if not all, of us here present have the privilege of being members. I am about to express my own sympathy, and to claim yours, for labours of his, as wrought for the common good, the spiritual profit of us all. For myself I need hardly say that there does not seem to me any inconsistency in this. I feel no embarrassment in the contemplation of the position which I occupy; nor am I conscious that any explanation, still less that any apology, is needful from me. When brought into contact with those who stand outside of our own communion, be they the living or the dead, I make no pretence of believing that there are not differences, it may be important differences, between us; I do not hesitate to profess that I regard my own as the best; else how should I justify my cleaving to it? And further, I am persuaded that we do not hasten, but rather put further off, that blessed day when all who are Christ's shall be outwardly as well as inwardly one in Him, by premature anticipations and snatchings at the same. To heal our divisions, so to heal them, I mean, that they shall not presently break out anew and prove more inveterate than ever, is almost a Pentecostal work. Whenever things are ripe for such a consummation, it will come as of itself; there will be no mistake about it; the dividing walls and separating barriers will fall away as of their own accord. Meanwhile, and having ever in view the hastening of the coming of such a day, there is a duty which is plainly ours, a duty at once negative and positive; a negative duty, that we do not accentuate, emphasize, exaggerate points of difference; a positive duty, that we heartily thank God for all which He has wrought *in* any of his Saints and servants, for the likeness to Christ which He has formed in them; and not less for all which He has accomplished *by* them; that we recognize this with no grudging recognition as a contribution thrown into the common stock of the Church, an addition to the wealth not of a section of it, but of the whole. It is this last duty, which it is my privilege and pleasure to be called to fulfil to-day. With Richard Baxter's Nonconformity, whether it was his fault, or the Church's fault, or nobody's fault, or everybody's fault, with this I have happily nothing this day to do. With these preliminary words I pass to my proper theme.

There are books which seem rather to write themselves, than to be written; which are as the medicinal gum that oozes from the tree, without constraint and almost without solicitation; books, of which the authors, if it were demanded of them why they wrote them, might with perfect truth reply, because they could not help it. Such I take very much 'The Pilgrim's Progress' to have been; and such 'The Imitation of Christ'; the literary purpose, the intention of composing a book, having altogether fallen into the background. Many passages make plain that Baxter's 'Saint's Rest' is a book of the same spontaneous birth; and I much regret that in the shorter form, which is the only one for the most part in which we possess or read it, these passages have mainly or altogether been allowed to disappear. For indeed, as is needful for many reasons here to observe, the veritable work, as it came from Baxter's hands, has important points of unlikeness as compared with the little volume, which we give as a prize in our Sunday schools, and in other ways seek to disperse; and which in the case of many among us is probably all with which we ourselves are familiar. In mere bulk, the book as he wrote and published it is four or five times bigger than the little volume which we know; so that when this announces itself as 'abridged,' this announcement fails to convey, or conveys very inadequately, the fact of the extent to which it has been cut short; nay, I am obliged to add, cut short not always with understanding. Thus, to go no further than the title-page, we miss there the affecting and very instructive words as to the true meaning and primary purpose with which it was written, 'Written by the Author for his own use, in the time of his languishing, when God took him off from all public employment.' And we miss not less many allusions to the troublous times in which he lived and wrote, to Worcester, and Edgehill, and Naseby, to the pall of mourning which our Civil War had spread over the face of England; all of which had their use, served to give an historic basis to the book, and hindered it from floating as it were in the air. I would not here be misunderstood. The process of abridgement has been somewhat mercilessly, and at times somewhat clumsily executed; and yet under no other conditions could the book have made itself the home which it has made in the hearts of so many thousands in our land. Half is sometimes more than the whole; and this may be true of the fourth part as well. The book, as Baxter wrote it, is long; sometimes, if we were to venture to speak out all that is in our hearts, we should acknowledge it is tedious; above all in the earlier parts. It is only after a while that he extricates himself from straits and narrows, in which he has needlessly entangled himself there.

But now having ventured on this word of fault-finding, let me finish with the same; and note certain defects and drawbacks, mostly formal, which, if I am not mistaken, cleave to it; that so, this done, I may dismiss the subject, and proceed to trace, as I best may, what of excellent worth it offers to us. Baxter then, a master in the art of the distribution of his materials, with many of the merits of the Schoolmen whom he studied so closely, and with some of their faults, sometimes abuses this mastery; pushes distinctions and divisions so far, multiplies them so wantonly, that not clearness, but confusion, is the result. His method is not his servant, but he the servant of his method. And as with the distribution of his materials, so also with his materials themselves. They accumulate beyond all reason under his hands. He is so full, with so vast a range of theological interests, so well versed in the controversies of his own time and of the times past, that it is only too easy for him to go off upon some side quest, if such offers itself to him, and to follow it up much further than is consistent with the main purpose or general symmetry of the work which he has actually in hand. Take a notable example of this from the book immediately before us. He has not advanced very far in his praise of the heavenly rest before it comes strongly home to him that the certainty of our inheriting this rest depends on the credibility of the Scriptures which promise it, on the fact that they are no other than the infallible word of God; and hereupon he addresses himself to the whole question of the divine authority of Scripture, and generally of the Evidences of the Christian Religion, devoting more than one hundred and thirty closely printed pages to the subject. I need hardly say that with occasional good points this treatise on Christian Evidences, for it is nothing less, is of comparatively little value now; although this by no fault of the writer. The battle which is of all the ages, that, I mean, of faith with unbelief, has within the last two hundred years, above all during the last twenty, so shifted its ground, that 'the high places of the field,' those which, being won or lost, do in fact determine the issues of the conflict, have ceased to be the same which in his time they were; nay the very foes are different, and different too is that for which *we* are contending. The Deist of the seventeenth century denied the *fact* of our having received a revelation from God; he never, so far as I know, denied the *possibility* of our receiving such a revelation. Then, and up to a recent date, we had not staked all upon the issue. Even if the battle had gone against us, something would have still remained; or at least we might have believed that something remained; a living personal extramundane God, governing the world in righteousness; a voice of conscience, his voice within us, attesting the everlasting distinctions between good and evil; the hope of immortality. These, with other things precious, men might still have counted their own. Now there is no room for any such belief; the conflict is for all which we have; for all which is human and all which is divine in man; and it is well that we should look this fact in the face.

And other avenues stretching away to the right hand and to the left, Baxter cannot always resist the temptation to explore; and this, though they may lead him far away from that which is his more immediate concern. Above all, let him only find himself in the neighbourhood of some perplexed question of the Schools, such a one as has tasked and divided the subtlest intellects of Christendom for centuries, which has set Thomist against Scotist, Realist against Nominalist, and is likely to do the same to the end of time;—for these controversies are not dead, they have only a little shifted their ground;—and at once, like the war-horse of Job, he smells the battle afar off, 'the thunder of the captains and the shouting,' and nothing will content him till he finds himself in their midst.

I have thus delivered myself freely in regard of certain drawbacks and faults from which this book cannot be affirmed to be free; and dealing, as I am thus far, mainly with things formal and external, let me mention here, before entering into deeper matters, one formal merit which it eminently possesses. I refer to that without which, I suppose, no book ever won a permanent place in the literature of a nation, and which I have no scruple in ascribing to it—I mean its style. A great admirer of Baxter has recently suggested a doubt whether he ever recast a sentence, or bestowed a thought on its rhythm, and the balance of its several parts; statements of his own make it tolerably certain that he did not. As a consequence he has none of those bravura passages which must have cost Jeremy Taylor, in his 'Holy Living and Dying' and elsewhere, so much of thought and pains, for such do not come of themselves, and unbidden, to the most accomplished masters of language. But for all this there reigns in Baxter's writings, and not least in 'The Saint's Rest,' a robust and masculine eloquence; nor do these want from time to time rare and unsought felicities of language, which, once heard, can scarcely be forgotten. In regard indeed of the choice of words the book might have been written yesterday. There is hardly one which has become obsolete; hardly one which has drifted away from the meaning which it has in his writings. This may not be a great matter; but it argues a rare insight, conscious or unconscious, into all which was truest, into all which was furthest removed from affectation and untruthfulness in the language, that after more than two hundred years so it should be; and we may recognize here an element, not to be overlooked, of the abiding popularity of the book.

Having tarried thus long as in the outer court of the temple, let me now draw nearer to the heart of things. And first I will attempt to realize to myself and to you the conditions, outward and inward, under which this book was produced, the forces which contributed to its production; for these will have gone far to make it what it is. I remarked at the outset that the book was one of those which seem rather to write themselves than to be written. Let this, however, be as it may, so much at least stands fast, that it was originally composed for his own use—surely an invaluable condition for a book of practical divinity, that it should have been written to instruct, to comfort, to strengthen him from whom it came, and then, if it might be, others. We have his own account of the genesis of the book, the pearl and crown, as I take it, of all his books. Removed by sickness from all active exercise of his ministry, left solitary in a country-house, sentenced to death by the physicians, 'I began,' he says, 'to contemplate more seriously the everlasting rest which I apprehended myself to be just on the borders of. That my thoughts might not too much scatter in my meditation, I began to write something on the subject; but being continued long in weakness, where I had no books and no better employment, I followed on till it was enlarged to the bulk in which it is published.'

This then we note first about the book, and as helping to explain and account for its existence, namely, that it was the writing of one whose own life was a long familiarity with pain; not seldom a strong agony; who could take up with most literal truth the words of the great apostle, 'In this tabernacle we groan.' No one would willingly read the catalogue which more than once he has given of all the diseases which laid siege in his body to the citadel of life; but certainly no one can read it without marvel that one with twenty mortal sicknesses on his head should have seen that suffering life prolonged for threescore and sixteen years. As little can any one read it without admiration for that continual triumph of the spirit over the flesh and over fleshly ills, which could alone have enabled him to crowd into years so preoccupied with pain such a vast amount of work for God. He makes no parade of these sufferings; in this book only slightly alludes to them; but the yearning of the sick after health, of the weary after rest, the sense of unease, of a vast weariness enfolding all things here, makes itself very distinctly felt in such passages as the following :—

'Surely, a man would think, who looks upon the face of the world, that rest should to all men seem seasonable. Some of us are languishing under continual weakness, and groaning under most grievous pains, crying in the morning, would God it were evening, and in the evening would God it were morning, weary of going, weary of sitting, weary of standing, weary of lying, weary of eating, of speaking, of walking, weary of our very friends, weary of ourselves; oh how oft hath this been mine own case, and is not rest yet seasonable? Whither can you go; or into what company can you come, where the voice of complaining doth not show that men live in a continual weariness? But especially the saints, who are most weary of that which the world cannot feel. What godly society almost can you fall into, but you shall hear by their moans that somewhat aileth them? Some weary of a blind mind, doubting concerning the way they walk in, unsettled in almost all their thoughts; some weary of a hard heart, some of a proud, some of a passionate, and some of all these and much more. Some weary of their daily doubtings and fears concerning their spiritual estate, and some of the want of spiritual joys, and some of the sense of God's wrath, and is not rest then seasonable?'

But, again, Baxter felt profoundly the religious

divisions, if not of Christendom, yet certainly of England; and moreover, as he himself often confesses, there was a deep disappointment which mingled with his sense of these. That the openly profane should make war with all who would live godly, for this he was prepared; nothing else was to be expected. But it went to his heart, and he recurs to this with a sad iteration, that those professing godliness should scorn and defame, should bite and devour one another as they did. Some of us may have heard tell of a dying saint, who being reminded by his friends that he was passing into a world where the wicked cease from troubling, took up and completed the patriarch's words, adding, 'Yes, and where the good cease from troubling too.' Few have felt this troubling on the part of the good, or of those whom he esteemed good, more acutely than Baxter did. I am confident that I do not err in esteeming it one of the main burdens which made him yearn for that heavenly rest, where the wicked cannot, and where the good have no desire, to trouble any more.

Some will be surprised when I thus implicitly claim Baxter as a son of peace; some will be tempted to disallow this claim; remembering, as no doubt they will, that he certainly took no inconsiderable share in the theological fighting of his time. And no doubt, at a first glance, and as long as we dwell on the mere surface of things, it is not unnatural to regard him as a man of war, of strife and contention all his life long; fighting against everybody; fighting, as I need not tell you, against Papists, though counted by many Protestants as only half-hearted in this battle, and this because he would not teach that the further from Rome the nearer to God; fighting against the Prelatists or Bishops; and then, when these had disappeared for a while from the scene, misliking many things in the Presbyterian rule which had succeeded; at open war with the Independents, with the Fifth Monarchy Men, with the Anabaptists; with the Libertines or Antinomians; with the Quakers, not the sober quietists then that they are now; with the Seekers, who counted that the kingdom of God was still to seek; and with various minor sects, 'some tolerable, some intolerable,' so he describes them, which distracted the land; his hand against all these; and yet I am bound to say, with all this, never in my judgment fighting for mere fighting's sake; but always fighting for peace. When he said, and they are words well worth remembering, ' He that is not a son of peace is not a son of God,' this was not merely a pointed epigrammatic saying which he was uttering, but a voice which came from the deep of his heart. And it is no more than due to him to add that as he yearned, so he laboured, for peace. There is something affecting, almost pathetic, in his entire confidence, a confidence which no experience seemed able to shake, that all men, if once shown they were in the wrong, would at once own that they were so, and without more ado would confess and forsake the errors of which they were convinced. In this conviction he was never weary of writing books with titles such as these: 'A Friendly Accommodation,' or again, 'Pacifying Principles,' or once more, 'Against Contentious and Church distracting Controversies,' or yet once again, 'An End of Doctrinal Controversies by reconciling Explication.'

Whether his schemes of at-one-ment were in deed always reconciling and pacifying may be fairly a question; but in this indomitable faith of his that peace was attainable, and that for the attaining of this it only needed that men should be clearly made to see on which side the right lay, and that it was possible to make them see this, I recognize a certain simplicity if you will; but the grand simplicity of a man who ascribed to others the same intellectual and moral honesty, the same allegiance to the truth, or to what they believed to be the truth, which he found in himself.

I have said that it might very fairly be a question whether his schemes of pacification were such as were always likely either in manner or matter to be crowned with very signal success. And indeed, when we come to acquaint ourselves a little closer with them, it is not very wonderful if they failed. Here is one of his summonses to the 'word-warriors'—this excellent phrase is of his own coining—to lay down their arms and to come to some understanding. It constitutes the title-page of his 'Catholic Theology,' and little as he may have intended this, it must be owned that every word of it is a provocation and a challenge. It is worth quoting, and with very slight omissions I quote it:—

'Catholic Theology, plain, pure, peaceable; for pacifying of the dogmatical word-warriors, who by contending about things unrevealed, or not understood, and by putting verbal differences for real, and their arbitrary notions for necessary sacred truths, deceived and deceiving, have long been the shame of the Christian religion, a scandal and hardening to unbelievers, the incendiaries, dividers and distracters of the Church, the subverters of their own souls, and those of their followers, calling them to a blind zeal and wrathful warfare against true piety, love and peace, and teaching them to censure, backbite, slander and prate against each other for things which they never understood.'

Certainly it is not strange if these words exercised no eminently pacifying influence on those to whom they were addressed; if he who wrote them had often to take up the words of the Psalmist: 'I labour for peace, but when I speak to them thereof, they make them ready to battle.' As I have said already, this dwelling in the tents of Kedar, this labouring for peace, but, whether by his own fault or the faults of others, labouring in vain, was another burden of his spirit, and one I am persuaded which mightily helped his longing for the true City of the Vision of Peace.

But if life had its disappointments, it had its dangers too; was full of these, of temptations innumerable. How should he not yearn to leave them for ever behind. Hear some words of his, and you will own that he took these temptations in earnest, that for him the conflict with them was not a mere beating of the air, or fighting with shadows:—

'O the hourly dangers that we poor sinners walk in! Every sense is a snare, every member a snare, every mercy a snare, and every duty a snare to us. We can scarce open our eyes but we are in danger. If we behold them above us, we are in danger of envy. If we see sumptuous buildings, pleasant habitations, honour and riches, we are in danger to be drawn away with covetous desires; if the rags and beggary of others, we are in danger of self-applauding thoughts and unmercifulness. If we see beauty, it is a bait to lust; if deformity, to loathing and disdain. We can scarcely hear a word spoken, but contains to us matter of temptation. Have we comeliness and beauty, what fuel for pride! are we deformed, what an occasion of repining! Have we strength of reason and gifts of learning, oh how hard it is not to be puffed up, to seek ourselves, to hunt after applause, to mislike the simplicity of Christ. Are we unlearned, and of shallow heads and slender parts, how apt then to despise what we have not, and if conceitedness and pride do but strike in, to become a leading troubler of the Church's peace under pretence of truth and holiness. Are we men of eminence, how hard to devote our power to his glory from whom we have received it. Are we inferior and subjects, how prone to grudge at others' pre-eminence, to bring all their actions to the bar of our incompetent judgment. Are we rich and not too much exalted; are we poor and not discontented. If we be sick, oh how impatient; if in health, how few and stupid our thoughts of eternity!'

But the author of 'The Saint's Rest' aims at something more than the disenchanting us from the love of this world, and from the minding of earthly things. This is but half, and the easiest half, of the task which he has set before him. 'To despise earth,' he has somewhere said, 'is easy to me, but not so easy to be acquainted and conversant in heaven.' This, as its name sufficiently declares, is the motive and final cause of the book—to assist and set forward, in himself first and then in others, this acquaintance with heaven, this conversation in heaven; to kindle, by meditation on heavenly things, above all of the heavenly rest, the cold affection towards these which he mourned in himself, which he saw too plainly in others; which who is there among us that does not feel in himself?

And here is indeed an explanation of the immense importance which he attached to meditation, of the prominence which he gave to it as a help, nay, almost as an exercise absolutely necessary for the strengthening and deepening of the spiritual life of the soul, with the most careful directions when and where and how this may be most profitably exercised, which he gives. Many, if I mistake not, are wont to regard this exercise of meditation with coldness and distrust, as a device for the promotion of a certain artificial piety and a transient excitement of the religious affections; much extolled and much practised in the Roman Catholic Church; and recently, with other questionable helps to devotion, borrowed from it by a few among ourselves. There cannot, however, be a greater mistake than this. It needs but a very slight acquaintance with the best Puritan divinity of the seventeenth century, with such books as Gurnall's 'Christian Armour,' with Bates' treatise on this very matter, above all with the writings of Baxter, and this one first of all, to dissipate any such notion.

The fourth and concluding portion of 'The Saint's Rest,' nearly three hundred pages, and constituting almost an independent work—for it has its own title-page, its own preface, its own dedication—is devoted exclusively to the urging of this duty, which he describes as 'the delightfullest task to the spirit, and the most tedious to the flesh, that ever men on earth were employed in.' I must needs consider it the most precious portion of the whole book, indeed he himself announces that all which went before was but as a leading up to this. But he shall himself describe this section of his work: 'a Directory,' he calls it, ' for the getting and keeping of the heart in heaven by the diligent practice of that excellent unknown duty of Heavenly Meditation; being the main thing intended by the author in the writing of this book, and to which all the rest is but subservient.' And on meditation, not merely as a help to the heavenly life, but as one which none may lawfully forego, he often expresses himself very strongly, as thus: 'That meditation is a duty of God's ordering I never met with a man that would deny. It is in word confessed to be a duty by all, but by the constant neglect denied by most.'

I have thus sought to trace very briefly the moral and spiritual factors, as they present themselves to me, which wrought together for the producing of this book; the leading objects and aims which the writer of it set before him. But what, some may say, to whom it is still an unknown land, or who to-day for the first time are skirting with me its outermost borders, what of special spiritual good may we hope to obtain by nearer acquaintance with it? First, then, let me say, If there should be any in this great assembly who, notwithstanding their presence among us here to-day, do yet in their heart of hearts think scorn of that pleasant land, are despisers of that heavenly rest to which he invites them, they, if they can be persuaded to a closer familiarity with it, will come into contact with one whom in other points they may judge of as they may; but this I dare affirm they will not be able to deny, that to him heaven was no sentimental dream, and hell no painted flame; with one who will plead with them as probably they never have been pleaded with before, lest a promise being left them of entering into that rest, they should fall short of it. For indeed I have sometimes thought that this *pathos*, this passionate earnestness, is the quality in Baxter wherein he is almost, if not altogether, without a peer. There have been others in other points his equals and his superiors. But I ask myself where I should find any other such pleading with souls, any other, 'Why will ye die?' which does not fall short of his.

I could not leave this unsaid, without leaving unsaid that which is most characteristic of the man and of the book. But I do not dwell on it any further. It is of the book as a help to the setting foward of the higher life in them who have already begun well, that it is my task to speak. If you ask me what help to this you may expect to find in it, I will say in the first place, counsels of excellent good sense, as serviceable to-day as on the day upon which they were first uttered; protests against mischievous exaggerations, whether on the right hand or on the left, you will meet with in abundance. Thus what can be better than this against those who taught (there are some who teach so nowadays), that men not merely may know, but *must* know the exact moment of their conversion, or have not been converted at all :—

'I will not enquire whether thou remember the time or the order of these workings of the Spirit. There may be much uncertainty and mistake in that. But I desire thee to look into thy soul, and to see whether thou find such works [of the Spirit] wrought within thee. And then, if thou be sure they are there, the matter is not so great though thou know not when or how thou camest by them.'

Or here again on what I will venture to call the very small religious value of tears :—

'Some soft and passionate natures may have tears at command, when one that is truly gracious hath none; yet is this Christian with dry eyes more solidly apprehensive and deeply affected than the other is in the midst of his tears; and the weeping hypocrite will be drawn to his sin again with a trifle, which the groaning Christian would not be lured to commit with crowns and kingdoms.'

Or once more, on the infinite and dangerous self-confidence so often to be seen in those who after long walking in darkness have suddenly caught a partial glimpse of the true light :—

'The first new strange apparition of light doth so amaze them, they think they are in the third heavens, when they are but newly passed from the suburbs of hell ; and are presently as confident as if they knew all things, when they have not half light enough to acquaint them with their own ignorance.'

Certainly these are good ; and it would be easy to multiply them a hundredfold; but there is more and better and higher behind. That pathos which I ascribed to Baxter just now does not manifest itself merely in those calls to the unconverted, full as those are of an inward bleeding compassion. There are passages not a few toward the end of the book, strains of the most passionate devotion, in which he seeks to initiate such as have yielded themselves to his guidance into the deeper mysteries of divine meditation, to furnish them with some of the materials on which the soul may work, to lead them upward and onward, step by step, from strength to strength, from glory to glory, to the contemplation of the glory of God. Take, for example, this. He has spoken of some motives to love, and proceeds :—

'But if yet thou feelest not thy love to work, lead thy heart further, and shew it yet more. Shew it the King of saints on the throne of his glory, who is the first and the last; who liveth and was dead. Draw near and behold Him. Dost thou not hear his voice? He that called Thomas to come near and to see the print of the nails, and to put his fingers into his wounds, He it is that calls to thee, Come near, and be not faithless but believing. Look well upon Him. Dost thou not know Him? Why, it is He that brought thee up from the pit of hell, and purchased the advancement which thou must inherit for ever. And yet dost thou not know Him? Why, his hands were pierced, his head was pierced, his side was pierced, his heart was pierced with the sting of thy sins, that by these marks thou mightest always know Him. Hast thou forgotten since He wounded Himself to cure thy wounds; and let out his own blood to stop thy bleeding? If thou know Him not by the face, the voice, the hands, if thou know Him not by the tears and bloody sweat, yet look nearer thou mayest know Him by the heart.

'Hast thou forgotten the time when thou wast weeping, and He wiped the tears from thine eyes? when thou wast bleeding, and He wiped the blood from thy soul? when pricking cares and fears did grieve thee, and He did refresh thee and draw out the thorns? Hast thou forgotten when thy folly did wound thy soul, and the venomous guilt did seize upon thy heart; when He sucked forth the mortal poison from thy soul, though therewith He drew it into his own? Oh how often hath He found thee sitting weeping like Hagar, while thou gavest up thy state, thy friends, thy life, yea, thy soul for lost; and He opened to thee a well of consolation, and opened thine eyes also, that thou mightest see it. How oft hath He found thee in the posture of Elias, sitting down under the tree forlorn and solitary, and desiring rather to die than to live; and He hath spread thee a table of relief from heaven, and sent thee away refreshed, and encouraged to his work. How oft hath He found thee in such a passion as Jonas, in thy peevish frenzy aweary of thy life; and He hath not answered passion with passion, though He might indeed have done well to be angry, but hath mildly reasoned thee out of thy madness, and said, Dost thou well to be angry, and to repine against Me? How often He hath set thee on watching and praying and repenting and believing, and when He hath returned, hath found thee fast asleep, and yet He hath not taken thee at the worst, but instead of an angry aggravation of thy fault, He hath covered it over with the mantle of love, and prevented thy overmuch sorrow with a gentle excuse, The spirit is willing, but the flesh is weak. How oft hath He been traduced in his cause or name, and thou hast (like Peter) denied Him, at least by thy silence, while He hath stood in sight; yet all the revenge He hath taken hath been a heartmelting look, and a silent remembering thee of thy fault by his countenance.'

And hear him once and only once more; as he rebukes with the same passionate earnestness those who, loving God, do not love Him better; who professing to seek, and in a sense seeking, a heavenly country, are yet unwilling to reach it, and to find themselves (all life's tempests past) in the Fair Havens of the eternal rest :—

'Ah foolish, wretched soul, doth every prisoner groan for freedom? and every slave desire his jubilee? and every sick man long for health? and every hungry man for food, and dost thou alone abhor deliverance? Doth the seaman long to see the land? Doth the husbandman desire the harvest? and the traveller long to be at home? and the soldier long to win the field? And art thou loth to see thy labours finished? and to receive the end of thy faith? and to obtain the things for which thou livest? Are all thy sufferings only seeming? have thy griefs and groans been only dreams? If they were, yet methinks we should not be afraid of waking; fearful dreams are not delightful. Or is it not rather the world's delights that are all mere dreams and shadows? Is not all its glory as the light of a glow-worm, a wandering fire; yielding but small directing light and as little comforting heat in all our doubtful and sorrowful darkness? Or hath the world in these its latter days laid aside its ancient enmity? Is it become of late more kind? Who hath wrought this great change, and who hath made this reconciliation? Surely not the great Reconciler. He hath told us in the world we shall have trouble, and in Him only we shall have peace. We may reconcile ourselves to the world (at our peril), but it will never reconcile itself to us. Oh foolish unworthy soul, who hadst rather dwell in this land of darkness than be at rest with Christ; who hadst rather stay among the wolves, and daily suffer the scorpion's stings, than to praise the Lord with the Host of heaven! If thou didst well know what heaven is, and what earth is, it would not be so.'

And the same yearning which uttered itself in this book, the firstfruits of his pen, written before half his earthly pilgrimage was finished, abode with him in strength to the last. Richard Baxter is not generally known as a poet; but a small volume of 'Poetical Fragments,' so he calls them, is one of the hundred and forty books, great and small, which acknowledge him for their author. One of these poems he calls his 'Valediction,' that also written at a time when he esteemed himself on the very borders of the heavenly country, though in fact some ten years more should elapse before that country was reached.

Let me cite as *my* valediction a few verses from this, as showing that age had not dulled his longing desire for the Heavenly rest; being such also as may fitly quicken our own desire after the same:—

What is the time that's gone,
And what is that to come?
Is it not now as none?
    The present stays not.
Time posteth, oh how fast,
Unwelcome death makes haste,
None can call back the past,
    Judgement delays not.
Though God brings in the light,
    Sinners awake not;
Because hell's out of sight,
    They sin forsake not.

Man walks in a vain shew;
They know, yet will not know,
Sit still, when they should go,
    But run for shadows;
While they might taste and know
The living streams that flow,
And crop the flowers that grow
    In Christ's sweet meadows.
Life's better slept away
    Than as they use it;
In sin and drunken play
    'Vain men abuse it.

Is this the world men choose,
For which they heaven refuse
And Christ and grace abuse,
    And not receive it?
Shall I not guilty be
Of this in some degree,
If hence God would me free,
    And I'd not leave it?
My soul, from Sodom fly,
    Lest wrath there find thee;
Thy refuge rest is nigh,
    Look not behind thee.

There 's none of this ado ;
None of the hellish crew,
God's promise is most true,
    Boldly believe it.
My friends are gone before,
And I am near the shore,
My soul stands at the door ;
    O Lord, receive it.
It trusts Christ and his merits;
    The dead He raises.
Join it with blessed Spirits,
    Who sing thy praises.

WORKS
BY
R. CHENEVIX TRENCH, D.D.

NOTES on the PARABLES of OUR LORD. Fourteenth Edition. 8vo. 12s.

NOTES on the MIRACLES of OUR LORD. Twelfth Edition. 8vo. 12s.

SYNONYMS of the NEW TESTAMENT. Ninth Edition, enlarged. 8vo. 12s.

BRIEF THOUGHTS and MEDITATIONS on SOME PASSAGES in HOLY SCRIPTURE. Third Edition. Crown 8vo. 3s. 6d.

On the STUDY of WORDS. Eighteenth Edition, revised. Fcp. 8vo. 5s.

ENGLISH PAST and PRESENT. Thirteenth Edition, revised and improved. Fcp. 8vo. 5s.

SELECT GLOSSARY of ENGLISH WORDS used formerly in senses different from the present. Fifth Edition, revised and enlarged. Fcp. 8vo. 5s.

PROVERBS and their LESSONS. Seventh Edition, enlarged. Fcp. 8vo. 4s.

On the AUTHORISED VERSION of the NEW TESTAMENT. Second Edition. 8vo. 7s.

LECTURES on MEDIÆVAL CHURCH HISTORY. Being the Substance of Lectures delivered at Queen's College, London. Second Edition, 8vo. 12s.

GUSTAVUS ADOLPHUS in GERMANY, and other **LECTURES** on the THIRTY YEARS' WAR. Second Edition, enlarged. Fcp. 8vo. 4s.

KEGAN PAUL, TRENCH, & CO., London.

Works by R. CHENEVIX TRENCH, D.D.—continued.

POEMS. Library Edition. In Two Volumes. Crown 8vo. 10s.

POEMS. Collected and arranged anew. New Edition. Fcp. 8vo. 7s. 6d.

COMMENTARY on the EPISTLES to the SEVEN CHURCHES in ASIA. Fourth Edition, revised. 8vo. 8s. 6d.

SACRED LATIN POETRY. Chiefly Lyrical. Selected and arranged for Use. Third Edition, corrected and improved. Fcp. 8vo. 7s.

STUDIES in the GOSPELS. Fifth Edition, revised. 8vo. 10s. 6d.

SELECTED SERMONS. Crown 8vo. 6s.

The SERMON on the MOUNT. An Exposition drawn from the Writings of St. Augustine, with an Essay on his merits as an Interpreter of Holy Scripture. Fourth Edition, enlarged. 8vo. 10s. 6d.

SHIPWRECKS of FAITH. Three Sermons preached before the University of Cambridge in May 1867. Fcp. 8vo. 2s. 6d.

An ESSAY on the LIFE and GENIUS of CALDERON. With Translations from his 'Life's a Dream' and 'Great Theatre of the World.' Second Edition, revised and improved. Extra fcp. 8vo. 5s. 6d.

PLUTARCH: his Life, his Lives, and his Morals. Second Edition, enlarged. Fcp. 8vo. 3s. 6d.

A HOUSEHOLD BOOK of ENGLISH POETRY. Selected and Arranged, with Notes. Fourth Edition, revised. Extra fcp. 8vo. 5s. 6d.

REMAINS of the late Mrs. RICHARD TRENCH. Being Selections from her Journals, Letters, and other Papers. New and Cheaper Issue. With Portrait. 8vo. 6s.

KEGAN PAUL, TRENCH, & CO., London.

www.ingramcontent.com/pod-product-compliance
Lightning Source LLC
Chambersburg PA
CBHW031904220426
43663CB00006B/759